Memory Improvement Through EFT Tapping

T0002813

Memory Improvement Through EFT Tapping

A Way to Boost Recall and Clarity

PETA STAPLETON

Toplight

Jefferson, North Carolina

ISBN (print) 978-1-4766-9293-7
ISBN (ebook) 978-1-4766-5059-3

LIBRARY OF CONGRESS AND BRITISH LIBRARY
CATALOGUING DATA ARE AVAILABLE

Library of Congress Control Number 2023007049

Front cover image © MoremarShutterstock

Printed in the United States of America

Toplight is an imprint of McFarland & Company, Inc., Publishers

*Box 611, Jefferson, North Carolina 28640
www.toplightbooks.com*

Praise for *Memory Improvement Through EFT Tapping: A Way to Boost Recall and Clarity*

In *Memory Improvement Through EFT Tapping: A Way to Boost Recall and Clarity*, Dr. Peta Stapleton seamlessly fuses EFT research with client stories and clear, practical tapping guidance to improve memory. Whether you want to improve your memory, or be less forgetful, or are a student looking to supercharge your learning, there is something for everyone in this book. Buy this guidebook now and remember to tap to improve your memory every day.

—Professor Liz Boath, PhD. Author
of *Making the Case for EFT and Energy Psychology: Designing, Conducting and Publishing Case Studies*

Emotional Freedom Technique (EFT) is a tool for coping with many forms of life stress. Much research connects stress and maladaptive ways of coping with cognitive health outcomes such as memory impairment and age-related cognitive decline. Dr. Stapleton is the leading scholar and practitioner in EFT, and she masterfully explains this research and shows you how to use EFT to cope successfully with life's challenges and protect your cognitive health. Importantly, the book elucidates the many mechanisms through which EFT can positively impact your life and improve your overall well-being with special attention to remaining mentally sharp and optimally functioning throughout your life.

—Professor Loren Toussaint, director
of Laboratory for the Investigation of Mind,
Body, and Spirit, Luther College, Iowa, USA

Many thanks to Dr. Peta Stapleton for offering such clear and concise guidance in her universally useful new book, *Memory Improvement Through EFT Tapping*. Learning how to release all the stress that interferes with our memory is beyond helpful—for ourselves and everyone we love. Peta's new book offers us a path to enjoy optimal memory at any age.

—Carol Look, LCSW, EFT Master, International
Workshop Leader, Abundance Coach, Author,
Attracting Abundance with EFT, www.CarolLook.com

Not only is Dr. Peta Stapleton one of the leading researchers in the field of EFT/Tapping, she is also fantastic at showing people how to make use of this simple yet effective tool in a variety of situations. *Memory Improvement Through EFT Tapping* is another great resource that she has made available—one that can be beneficial for pretty much anyone. While the primary focus is on strengthening one's memory, it is also a valuable aid for managing other uncomfortable consequences of stress. This book will improve much more than just your memory.

—Brad Yates, tapwithbrad.com

In *Memory Improvement Through EFT Tapping*, Peta offers a concise overview of the main factors that limit and reduce our memory, and then a simple stress reduction technique to assist. The application of EFT Tapping for memory issues is outstanding, and the fact that it can be offered to young children during their education years, to other areas such as remembering people's names and even learning a new language, means everyone needs this book.

—Pedro Gondim, CEO
(Mental Health Academy)

Another brilliant book by Dr. Peta Stapleton. *Memory Improvement Through EFT Tapping* is filled with clear and concise research, as well as examples for how to use tapping/EFT in the moment, to help reduce stress, and ultimately help you retain information in your brain and remember where you left your keys (and why you walked into a room, amongst other things)! She uses practical and easy-to-apply suggestions to help you feel like you are empowered by your mind, not as though you are losing it. The results are consistently and astoundingly effective, as I have used it myself many times (personally and with clients). I have been tapping for well over 25 years and I am forever a student to keep learning how we can use tapping to improve our lives. I highly recommend this book and suggest you keep it handy ... you will refer to it over and over again!

—Julie Schiffman, MSW, Tapping Expert

What I love best about Dr. Peta Stapleton's work is how straightforward and practical her work is. *Memory*

Improvement Through EFT Tapping is another perfect example of this approach. Even as a practitioner who has been working with clients for over 15 years, I found new practical approaches to understanding the issues around memory and simple straightforward ways to transform these issues. *Memory Improvement Through EFT Tapping* is a must-read for those new to tapping as it will hold your hand in a step-by-step so that you can achieve the results you want and for those who have been tapping for years as the book [includes] loads of golden nuggets of wisdom that you add to your more advanced practice.

—Gene Monterastelli, editor
of TappingQandA.com

This is an important and timely book in light of our aging population and increased stress levels. Peta very clearly explains the science and up-to-date information on memory and stress. There are so many valuable examples and applications everyone can easily use and benefit from. EFT reduces stress and improves memory; as an EFT practitioner I see this in my clinic every day.

—Louise Sage, Advanced Clinical EFT
Practitioner, Trainer & Mentor

This is a must-have handbook for life! Who wouldn't want to preserve or improve their memory when memory is the basis of daily functioning? The interactive chapters will not only teach you how to improve your memory but will impart a deeper understanding of the things that impact memory in a negative way and how to use EFT to change what may be holding you back.

—Michelle McCosker, Clinical EFT
Practitioner, Trainer & Mentor

To those who enter the World Memory
Championships—you are truly amazing.

Author's Note

Although they are gaining in scientific support, Emotional Freedom Techniques (EFT) and "tapping" are still considered experimental in nature. All information in this book is intended to promote awareness of the benefits of learning and applying EFT. However, the general public must take full responsibility for their use of it. The material in this book is for your general knowledge only and is not a substitute for traditional medical attention, counseling, therapy, or advice from a qualified health-care professional.

Neither EFT nor the information here is intended to be used to diagnose, treat, cure, or prevent any disease or disorder. Please note that if you begin tapping and find yourself overwhelmed, distressed, or becoming aware of previously forgotten memories, you may need to seek the professional help of a trained and experienced EFT practitioner.

A lack of results or progress may also mean you need professional assistance. If you have any concern regarding your health or mental state, it is recommended that you seek out advice or treatment from a qualified, licensed health-care professional. Before making any changes to your diet, medication, or health plan, it is recommended that you first consult with a doctor, pharmacist, or other qualified medical or health professional.

Note: All names and identifying details of real clients have been changed to protect their privacy.

Table of Contents

Acknowledgments

This journey started when I was reading *Moonwalking with Einstein: The Art and Science of Remembering Everything* (by Joshua Foer). I was so intrigued by the memory exercises in that book and the Memory Championships that occur worldwide, that I immediately saw the application of tapping for memory that could complement this. While many skilled practitioners were using tapping to assist clients, no one had written about all the applications here. I had been teaching students to use tapping for study habits and in exam settings, but no book existed. And so, this book was born! (Many thanks to Joshua for unknowingly planting the seed.)

As the African proverb says, it takes a village to raise a child. In this case it is the book that is the child! I owe thanks to many. To the leaders in the tapping field, who share their case studies and ideas and allow me to badger them with questions. They also embrace the research we conduct and share it far and wide. To my clients and students, who entertain my ideas and welcome tapping into their lives. They asked the questions you see answered throughout this book and allowed me to refine my answers.

To my family members, who don't even raise an eyebrow when I announce, "I'm writing another book." They might roll their eyes when I suggest tapping for the upcoming exam or to remember someone's name, but not when I am holed up in my office writing. I even sought their expertise in what they find hard to remember and what type of memory (beliefs) they thought they had. Thank you for always supporting my passion for tapping.

Thank you to my business partner Kate, who willingly read every chapter and made suggestions along the way. She has an eye for detail that is a godsend when I have read a chapter so many times I can't see the errors anymore. Kate shared her wisdom in her own journey as a daughter with a parent suffering cognitive decline and how she used tapping to support this. Kate and I met by chance (is anything just by chance?) and now co-direct Mind Heart Connect, an organization that raises awareness of mind-body-heart connections through evidence-based practices. You can see the details of events and trainings they offer at *https://mindheartconnect.com/* and the foundation arm that has a special focus on addressing the impact of immediate and intergenerational trauma in Aboriginal and Torres Strait Islander and refugee communities with tapping at *https://mindheartconnect.org/.*

To the team at McFarland Publishers and Toplight Books. Thank you for coming on this journey to share the applications of memory improvement through EFT Tapping!

And finally, thanks to you, the reader, for embracing this stress-reduction technique and being willing to engage. Research into and application of tapping have come a long way in the last four decades, and the more people who use it and talk about it, the more you will notice how common tapping is! It is part of my dream that schools will teach tapping to all students, that no one will think twice about tapping for their stress. Imagine a world where people know how to identify if they are stressed, and then can easily reduce it with tapping—that's the world I want to be in.

Stay open everyone, and enjoy your fantastic memory!

Introduction

Have you ever walked into a room and stopped, wondering *why* you walked in there? Have you ever bumped into someone you knew and could not remember their name? Have you ever sat for a test or exam and, even though you knew the material, in that very (inopportune) moment a fact or concept escaped you?

I could go on. These common everyday occurrences are just that—common. They happen to everyone at some stage. Memory seems to be a changing entity: it works for us one minute and fails us the next! We might even convince ourselves that, as we age, memory is expected to worsen: "Oh, you are just getting older. You are bound to forget things."

What if I told you there was something that could not only help with memory issues such as those mentioned above but also help prevent more serious memory-related issues such as confusion and dementia? If you could learn a way to keep your mind and body and, ultimately, your brain calm and focused so your memory was outstanding, would you be open to that?

Several decades ago I came across a stress-reduction technique that you apply to yourself, and it seems to work for a wide range of issues. You may know what it feels like to be stressed when sitting for that exam or giving that speech, but cognitive overload (having too much on your mind) that causes you to forget where you put your keys—or that friend's name—is also a form of stress. All types of stress can affect your memory and your ability to remember names, recall facts, remember where you put the keys, and even someone's name.

So, would you be open to reducing stress in order to have a fantastic memory? And if I told you children as young as five years old could also do this stress-reduction method, would that be of interest? If any teenagers in your house or life knew how to stay calm during a test and how to access those facts they studied, would that make your life easier too?

Here's how one of my students benefited.

Maddison was a bright and eager student when she started her university studies. But just the sheer volume of work that she needed to do each week started to impact her. She found herself working late into the night, often only getting four hours' sleep, and she was not eating or focusing well. Even though she was studying for hours, she could not retain the information, and her grades started declining. She was distracted and confused even when doing simple tasks and forgot her pet's name when she went to visit her parents one weekend. They were very worried about her and thought perhaps she might have something seriously wrong. A visit to the doctor ruled out anything more serious than stress. Maddison went to visit someone to teach her the stress-reduction technique in this book, and within weeks she was much calmer. She couldn't believe that she was putting less time into her studies and workload but achieving better grades. She remembered everything she studied (and everyone's names!), and the only thing that was different was her new calm.

A Stress-Reduction Technique

The approach I am talking about is called Emotional Freedom Techniques (EFT) or "tapping." We call it tapping because it describes what we do—physically tap with two fingers on acupressure points on the body. Tapping uses acupressure points similar to those perhaps familiar with acupuncture—we just don't use any needles!

Tapping is a rapidly growing field in the self-help area, but only in the last decade has it become the focus of clinical and scientific trials to test its effectiveness. To date, we have more than 300 research studies published in professional, peer-reviewed journals, but many people may not be familiar with this body-based stress-reduction technique—yet.

Recent research has used modern scientific techniques and instruments, such as DNA changes, brain scans, stress hormone (cortisol) testing, and brain waves, to study how the use of tapping helps with a wide range of emotional and physical issues. Tapping has now been formally recognized by Veterans Affairs (USA), the Canadian Psychotherapy Association, the National Institute for Health and Care Excellence (UK), and the National Disability Insurance Scheme (Australia). We have a wealth of "proof" that tapping works and is accepted.

With age comes the increasing likelihood of developing memory loss, and approximately 40 percent of adults 65 years or older do have age-associated memory impairment. However, it is also well established that stress, anxiety, or depression can cause forgetfulness, confusion, difficulty concentrating, and other problems that disrupt daily activities. Research suggests we *can* change memory impairments caused by stress—and tapping is a perfect solution.

My goal in this book is to teach you this extremely effective stress-reduction tool and outline how tapping can be used to address memory issues. We'll cover how the technique can remedy minor everyday issues such as forgetfulness, supercharge learning processes in students, and even be used for conditions such as dementia.

The Outline of This Book

This book is a comprehensive mix of "how to do" practical applications of tapping, real client stories from our work, and outcomes from the research. Each chapter gives you the exact ways to use tapping for that topic. My ultimate goal is for you to release stress for optimal memory, learning, and wellness. You can choose to read the chapter that interests you, or proceed from cover to cover. I highly recommend you read Chapter 1 first to learn the technique and also visit *www.petastapleton.com/memorybook* to download a handout of the tapping points and the process.

On that webpage there are videos to learn the technique visually that are appropriate for anyone 12 years or older. You can watch me do tapping and see the ways it is applied to different concerns at *www.petastapleton.com/memorybook*.

As mentioned, Chapter 1 will teach you what tapping is and how to do it. It is a practical chapter with some simple examples of using tapping for everyday memory issues, and you could start straight away after reading. (Chapter 4 shows you a variation of tapping to use with younger children.) If you are interested in more of the history about tapping, where it came from, and the key research to support it, my book *The Science Behind Tapping: A Proven Stress Technique for the Mind and Body* (Hay House, 2019) is for you.

Chapter 2 is all about how stress can affect memory and how tapping helps with this. I offer you some easy ways to understand how stress has this impact, which makes it easier to then accept how reducing stress may improve memory. There is a section on applying tapping directly to everyday stress in this chapter and a brief overview of the research that shows how tapping results in an enormous decrease in cortisol (the stress hormone) after just one hour.

Chapter 3 is possibly my favorite: it covers how to use tapping for everyday memory issues such as forgetfulness. I show you what I do when I walk into a room and wonder why I did, and how I find things I have "lost." Read about real cases of people who use tapping for these issues and use the tip sheet provided online to keep track of what you tap on.

Chapter 4 is for students and dives deep into how tapping can be used for supercharged learning. From studying to sitting for an exam, retaining more of what you read when you do and remembering everyday things such as people's names, this chapter is useful for everyone from children just starting school to teens and adults. There are real stories here too of students who use discreet forms of tapping in public places (e.g., during the exam), and I show you how to do that. The adaptations we make to tapping for younger children are also outlined in this chapter.

Chapter 5 offers ways tapping has been used for memory loss and aging. There are specific suggestions for what to address with tapping here (e.g., those beliefs we might adopt that aging automatically leads to memory loss!). This chapter is for anyone wanting to change these issues.

Chapter 6 discusses three areas that are known to impact memory: sleep habits, how much exercise you do, and how much sugar you eat. Unfortunately, research does tell us that not enough sleep affects your memory, and too much sugar intake is linked to reduced memory and brain volume. The good news is that physical exercise can improve cognitive abilities and enhance your mood. But if any of these three areas are not optimal in your life right now, this chapter will show you how to use tapping to change them.

Chapter 7 targets three other areas known in the research to impact memory: alcohol use, smoking, and blood pressure. Each of these is discussed in terms of how tapping can be used to reduce consumption, gain more control (without willpower!), or even quit completely. Tapping has been explored in clinical trials for these areas, and the outcomes consistently show that you can reduce urges for substances and impact the body's systems in positive ways.

Chapter 8 outlines real-life cases of individuals who have used tapping for memory disorders such as Alzheimer's disease and dementia. There has been some research conducted in this area, and I outline the methods and outcomes.

Chapter 9 is designed to set you up from here and offers a plan for you to keep using tapping as you finish the book, including something called the Personal Peace Procedure. There is also a tapping plan for life for all ages available to download and complete after reading this chapter at *www.petastapleton.com/memorybook*.

Chapter 10 answers all the frequently asked questions about tapping and tells you what to do if you find that tapping does not seem to be working. If you have a question that comes to mind as you are reading the previous chapters, you may find it here! Feel free to jump to this section to have it answered immediately.

The end of the book offers practical resources and tapping giants to follow if you are eager to explore further. If you do want to know more about research and the evidence, there are several leading websites included here.

I hope you enjoy reading *Memory Improvement Through EFT Tapping* and make the practical plan part of your everyday life. We always want to hear your stories too (see end of book to make contact). When I see my students sitting in the exams I have written and watch them discreetly tapping to recall my lectures and what I have taught them, I have to chuckle. I also see the light-bulb memory moment in those exams when they remember what they wanted to write, and it warms my heart. What a gift to be able to calm your mind and body (even without anyone knowing) and bring your memory back online! This book is my gift to your memory, and to children and teens in your life. Now let's get tapping.

CHAPTER 1

What Tapping Is
and How to Do It

EFT stands for Emotional Freedom Techniques and is considered a brief psychological strategy that combines a thinking element and a physical one. EFT uses the physical activity of tapping with two fingers on acupressure points on the face and body, while stating the psychological problem out loud (your thought).[1] Hence it is often called "tapping."

Tapping is, simply, a stress-management or regulation tool, which is usually self-applied. It is designed to calm the body's physiological systems so you may be able to think more clearly, gain clarity or perspective, or just feel calmer. And, of course, it can assist with improving memory!

Dawn, an 80-year-old client of EFT Trainer and Advanced Practitioner Naomi Janzen, surprised and impressed at the results she'd experienced with her chronic back pain, quipped, "Can it help with my memory?" She was joking but took note when Naomi replied, "Give it a try." Several months later Naomi ran into her on the street and asked her how her back was. She waved this away almost dismissively, more excited to say, "I've been using it to do crossword puzzles!" Her eyes shone with glee as she told Naomi she now taps her way through them every day and completes them in half the time it used to take.

Naomi had known EFT could help improve memory to the extent that stress was impacting general recall ability, but it hadn't occurred to her to use tapping in such an immediate and practical way. This was a case of a client teaching the practitioner something!

* * *

I am hoping now you need to know more about tapping!

The Tapping Technique

Acupressure or acupuncture points on the face and upper body are tapped upon with two fingers, usually the index and middle fingers. The strength of tapping should be comfortable, and you may be able to feel a reverberation spreading out across the adjacent area of your body from the point you are tapping. But if you don't, that is fine. It is recommended that you tap on each spot approximately seven times before moving on to the next spot, but you don't need to count these as you will instead be focusing on the words you are saying.

Typically, a person only uses tapping if they have a feeling or a thought they wish to change (usually a negative one). While it can be used for instilling positive emotional states or beliefs, this is only done when a negative state is minimized.

The Recipe

There are five easy steps to tapping.

1. First you acknowledge there is something you wish to change and subjectively rate that distress/discomfort out of 10 (10=most distress, 0=no distress). This is called a subjective unit of distress (SUDS) and is your internal "guess" as to the intensity of your problem. The aim is to tap until you feel calmer, or until your number might be 0–1, or you can stop if you have achieved the shift you want for that tapping time.

2. Then you state your problem in a setup statement (see below) while tapping on the side of the hand point (see diagram). This is usually done out loud so you stay engaged. You can state it in your mind, but you may be more likely to drift in your thoughts.

3. Then you tap through all eight acupressure points on the face and upper body while saying a short reminder phrase to keep your mind engaged. This is usually one or two words that just describe your feeling from the setup statement. The eight points are called a "round" in tapping.

4. Then take a breath and re-rate your distress out of 10. Remember, this is your guess.

5. Then keep tapping more rounds (through the face and upper body points) until you would guess your rating is quite low—a 1 or 0.

How It Looks

When you say the setup statement, you tap on the side of the hand, with two fingers from the other hand.

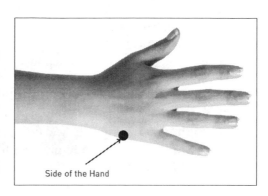

Figure 1A. Side of the Hand tapping point.

Side of the Hand

The Eight EFT Points on the Face and Upper Body

Figure 1B. The tapping points on the body

The Setup Statement

The typical setup statement has always been "Even though I [insert your feeling/issue here], I deeply and completely accept myself." You say this three times while tapping on the side of the hand point. This is to allow you to focus on what is happening and stay in the present moment.

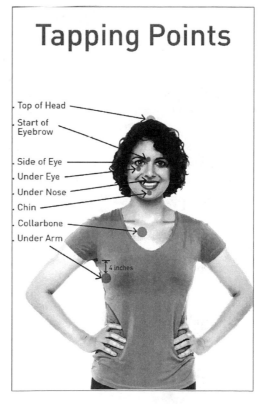

Tapping Points

Top of Head

Start of Eyebrow

Side of Eye

Under Eye

Under Nose

Chin

Collarbone

Under Arm

4 inches

9

But you can change that ending part. It is most important to state what the actual problem or feeling is, and then accept that this is how you feel *right now* (but you are going to change it, of course, through your tapping).

So, with that in mind, you could say any of the following at the end of the setup statement:

"Even though I ... I accept I have this problem."

"Even though I ... I am still a good person."

"Even though I ... I am taking charge right now."

"Even though I ... I want to change this."

"Even though I ... I completely and sincerely accept myself."

"Even though I ... I deeply and completely accept myself."

"Even though I ... I completely love/like and accept myself."

"Even though I ... I deeply and completely love and accept myself anyway."

"Even though I ... I deeply and completely forgive myself."

"Even though I ... I deeply and completely love and accept my feelings."

"Even though I ... I choose to love and accept myself."

"Even though I ... I choose to be open to this process."

"Even though I ... I am OK and open to the process."

"Even though I ... right here, right now, I am safe."

You start by saying your problem in this setup statement, but you accept that you have the problem with the end of the statement.

This is the difference with tapping compared to traditional therapy approaches: you acknowledge your problem by facing it. (This is actually similar to being very present to it, like in mindfulness.) The physical tapping aspect, however, helps calm the part of the brain sending out the response.

The short reminder phrase you say on each acupressure point is just the main feeling or negative state you want to change (e.g., "angry" or "sad").

The eight points in order are:

- eyebrow
- side of eye
- under eye
- under nose
- chin

- collarbone
- under arm
- top of head

An Example Related to Memory

Imagine you walk into a room and cannot quite recall what you wanted to do there (this is a common situation, as mentioned earlier!). You could say: "Even though I can't remember why I walked into this room, I am open to remembering."

Your reminder phrase would be "can't remember." This is the feeling you would rate out of 10 to start and see how it changes as you tap through the eight acupoints, as this is your actual problem.

As you complete a round of tapping, always ask yourself, "How intense (0 to 10) is the problem now?" (Has the intensity gone up or down?) This is your feedback about what is happening with the tapping. Mostly we notice that the SUDS goes down, but every now and then after the first round of tapping, you might notice that it increases. This usually means you have truly tuned into the problem (often for the first time), and this is the place to start. It does not mean tapping has not worked; it just means the true SUDS is the increased number: start from there.

Continue tapping if you are guessing the SUDS is still above a 0 or 1 after a few rounds. You can adjust the reminder phrase if you think of a better description as you tap. Maybe you start with tapping on feeling "angry" but after a few rounds you feel more "disappointed."

Another Example

Imagine you feel angry about something that just happened at work and you rate it 9 out of 10.

You tap on the side of the hand while saying "Even though I feel really angry right now, and I feel sick, I accept that I feel this way."

You do this three times while tapping on the side of the hand point.

Then you start tapping through the eight points above and say "so angry" or "I feel angry."

You would keep tapping until you felt a shift or difference, usually indicated by a low number out of 10.

So Why Do We Say the Negative?

This is a common question since many therapies seek to reframe a person's issue or simply get them to learn to accept it. Tapping does not affirm or implant a problem, although on the surface it may look like that. The process does have someone state the *truth* of what is happening for him or her and acknowledge it. We are actually engaging the amygdala (stress center) and the limbic system (emotions) in the brain and body with this technique.

It is as though we are engaging just enough with a level of distress to feel it, then we hit the delete button (through the tapping).

It is the tapping process that calms the physiological response from the body. Once this is released, cognitive shifts (or reframes as to how you view the situation now) may surface naturally.

If we tap with a positive affirmation first (attempting to take our mind off our problem), it may only result in a minor shift. It is like spraying air freshener when the garbage is still there. We need to tap on the real problem and reduce it before tapping on anything positive. There is more on how to tap on the positive later in this chapter.

The key in tapping is to actually do the tapping when you acknowledge your problem and state it out loud. It is the physical aspect that changes the response, not just stating your problem. We now know through research that the tapping aspect is a key active ingredient in the process working. Just stating your problem with an acceptance element may not result in it changing.

Very Briefly—How Does EFT Work?

Tapping appears to affect the amygdala (stress center in the brain) and hippocampus (memory center), and both play a role in the decision process when you decide if something is a threat. Tapping has also been shown to lower levels of cortisol, the stress hormone. Too much cortisol can result in lowered immune function and ultimately affect our physical health (e.g., fatigue, illnesses). This will all be discussed in later chapters.

12

Stimulation of acupoints like those used in tapping is believed to send a signal to the limbic or emotion system in the body and reduce its arousal.[2] This is why you tend to feel calmer after tapping. It is also why some people yawn while tapping!

Tapping can also decrease activity in the amygdala, which is part of the brain's arousal pathway.[3] And studies with long-term follow-up points are showing that the changes last over time, so there may be changes in the brain's neural pathways,[4] and different wiring can occur.

So, ultimately, we have this stress-management tool, a way of calming the body and brain to allow for clearer thoughts and solutions to present themselves. This is why it is such a wonderful tool for boosting memory and concentration and banishing forgetfulness, stress, and worry.

The Importance of Being Specific in Tapping

Tapping works best when you are very specific. Tapping on great, big, global statements such as "I forget everything" may not result in much change to your behavior. It is better to pick exact memories of past instances of forgetfulness and tap on what happened and how you felt. Pick the earliest possible memory as much as possible as this may be closer to the start of the behavior/pattern. You can also try to remember learning a behavior/pattern when you were quite young (e.g., by watching a family member). You can still tap on those times where you took on a lesson from someone else.

In tapping, there are often many pieces of the puzzle for an issue. Each piece may have several sides and these are called aspects. Those more critical to completing the picture are called core issues. When some parts are put together, the rest fall into place; this is called generalization.

What this means is that someone may have a lifetime of memories involving procrastination, for example. They just do it all the time. Tapping on specific events when procrastination was significant will be important. But it might not be necessary to tap on every instance of procrastination (you may sigh in relief here!). It only appears important to tap on the really significant memories you recall about the topic. It is like procrastination is the tabletop, and the individual memories are the legs of the table. You may only need to collapse the largest legs for the table to fall over.

Here is an example of a tabletop of someone who believes they have a poor memory in general. You can see that the legs of the table are examples of specific things in their life where they had something happen to let them know they had a poor memory. You may be doing your tapping on these individual legs as you become aware of them, and over time the belief of "I have a poor memory" will change and you will have a different reality.

Table Tops and Table Legs Example

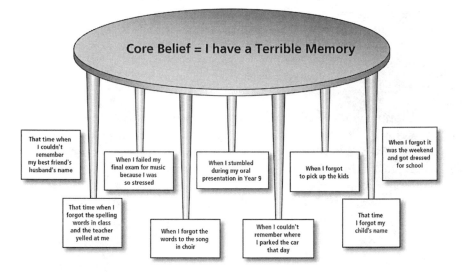

That time when I couldn't remember my best friend's husband's name

When I failed my final exam for music because I was so stressed

When I stumbled during my oral presentation in Year 9

When I forgot to pick up the kids

When I forgot it was the weekend and got dressed for school

That time when I forgot the spelling words in class and the teacher yelled at me

When I forgot the words to the song in choir

When I couldn't remember where I parked the car that day

That time I forgot my child's name

Figure 1C. Possible aspects related to a belief

Let's Look More at Aspects

A fear of public speaking may have the following aspects:

- the fear of being in front of an audience
- the fear of forgetting
- the worry you'll be embarrassed
- a tightness in your throat and chest
- worry about freezing up and not speaking at all

- a past memory of public speaking where something went wrong
- family stories of other people's public speaking humiliation

Aspects could be thoughts, feelings, bodily sensations, sounds, smells, or anything else you think of—we think of them as jigsaw pieces that all come together to make up a state or memory. In a distressing moment they tend to all blend together, and it can become harder to remember what actually happened. Tapping does help pull them apart, however, and reveal what was stored in that memory. It also explains why someone can smell something or hear a sound and be transported back in time, feeling as though a remembered experience is happening in the present. They may not recall that sound or smell from the original memory, but it is a trigger for it because it is stored as an aspect.

All of these things may need to be tapped on for the issue to be resolved. It may not take that long, though. Tapping can work quickly and can often be so fast it takes your breath away. The important thing is to keep tapping if you feel distressed; it is the tapping process that calms the limbic system and will help you stop crying, for example.

Positive Tapping?

Most people only tap when they feel a negative feeling they would like to reduce or discharge. You can also use tapping for positive statements, however. As mentioned, it is highly recommended you only do this after you have reduced any negative feelings associated with a memory, thought, or feeling. You can then do some rounds of positive tapping to instill any new feeling or belief you would like to have.

Examples

After you tap on feeling nervous about the test you have next week, you could then do a round of tapping on "Even though I was really nervous about that test coming up, I now feel calm and confident" (you can use "calm and confident" as the reminder phrase).

After you have tapped to reduce a stressed feeling, you could do a round of tapping on "Even though I was feeling stressed, I now feel calm and relaxed" (the reminder phrase is "calm and relaxed").

After you tap on not remembering people's names after the first time you meet them, you could tap a round or two with the words "Even though I couldn't remember that person's name just now, I am staying open to remembering" (the reminder phrase is "open to remembering").

Using "I Choose" Statements

Dr. Patricia Carrington[5] pioneered the "I choose" statements to help make the beneficial changes from EFT become permanent and generalize to many aspects of your life. You can add "I choose" to the end of the setup statement.

Examples

- "Even though I think I have a terrible memory for names, I choose to be open to change."
- "Even though I hate exercising, I choose to be fit and healthy."
- "Even though I'm nervous about that event next week, I choose to be calm and confident."

You will still tap on the actual problem (e.g., "I have a terrible memory for names") but the choice element at the end of the setup statement allows you to begin to choose a different story.

Before we end, I wanted to share a story of how tapping solved a problem of forgetting lines in a play for a young drama class student who "always" forgot her lines. It was just before the play was going to start, and she was in a nervous state about not remembering what she was supposed to say. Here is what EFT practitioner Mark Lawrence did.

* * *

Yesterday, my son's high school drama class put on a play. Half an hour before the play I noted a very nervous looking girl sitting on the grass copying her lines onto her palms.

I said, "That's cheating." She said, "I always forget my lines. I totally can't do this."

I sat down on the grass facing her and asked, "Do you want to fix that? We can fix it right now." She looked confused, of course, but agreed.

This was a far from ideal environment; there were about 15 to 20 excited teenagers running all around us burning off steam and generally making the kind of noise that only teenagers can make. Nonetheless, with more faith in EFT than in my intuitive skills in such a busy environment, we started.

As is my habit now, I gave her no introduction to EFT, not even the name. From her point of view, I was some strange guy who was going to have her do some very strange pantomime.

First I put a finger on my Sore Spot [under collarbone—sometimes used instead of side of the hand for setup statement] and said to her, "Find this spot. It's about here, it's a bit softer and deeper, and it feels a bit sore when you push on it." She found it quickly.

I told her to push hard enough that it was uncomfortable, but we didn't need real pain.

Then I had her say three times:

"Even though I get nervous and forget my lines, I deeply and completely respect and love myself."

With all the running around and talking near me, I found I was completely unable to get any sense at all of how we were doing. I had to just blindly trust the procedure, just as she was blindly trusting me.

Then I had her tap on the EFT points while repeating "forgetting my lines." I felt very unsatisfied by my own lack of feedback from my feelings about how she was doing, but I realized in this environment I had done everything I could.

So I told her with great confidence, "You're going to be fine now."

She asked what we had done. I told her it was kind of a modern version of acupuncture, except without needles. She then got up off the grass, her transcription score-to-palm chore forgotten, and ran around with the other kids.

After the play, she came up to me twice, about 10 minutes apart, all excited, and said, "I didn't forget a single line! Thank you!"

While I would hate to attempt to work on a more serious issue in such a distracting environment, I have to say that due to the power of EFT and the plasticity of youth, this experiment was a complete success.

* * *

So that brings us to the end of this chapter. Because it is often helpful to know what to do next, I have included some quick action steps you can take. Pause for a moment and see if you can do one of these today, before reading on to learn how stress can affect memory, concentration, and focus—and of course how tapping can help. Now, just about everyone would benefit from that!

Quick Action Steps

1. Revisit the tapping points image and tap on each point, and just take a comfortable breath on each. Just this activity (tap and breathe) can help regulate the body and make you feel calmer.

2. Complete this statement: "I believe I have a ... memory." Save this belief for some tapping as you read on.

CHAPTER 2

How Stress and Depression Can Affect Memory

If I asked you right now whether you have ever felt stressed in your life, I could probably bet everyone would say "yes"! Who, I hear you asking, hasn't felt stressed? Given the previous chapter outlined what tapping is—a stress-reduction technique—it would be remiss of me not to share how this approach actually lowers cortisol (the stress hormone). But first let's unpack exactly what stress is and how it might impact your memory.

Stress as a concept is both a physiological (physical) state and psychological response to something that has happened. It is also a process between you and the environment. If you believe something that has happened is threatening to you, harmful in any way, or believe it exceeds your ability to cope, then we tend to judge it as stressful. Our bodies might then respond by entering a fight or flight response (more on this later). Our response is that we feel "stressed out," and the process is that we will keep checking over time if anything has changed to decide if we can relax.

When we encounter any event (person or situation), we might ask ourselves, "What does it mean to me? Will I be OK?" We then ask: Is it irrelevant? Good (benign-positive)? Stressful?

We are always internally asking ourselves: "What kind of harm or loss might this situation cause me?" The ongoing process discussed above then happens. We may not be consciously aware of doing this decision-making. It can actually just happen unconsciously, out of conscious thought, but it is typically influenced by how we learned to cope with stress during our childhood. We watch our parents or main caregivers as a child, and because we are in a brain wave or rhythm state of being very open and almost hypnotic, we absorb everything around us as real.[1] Researchers actually call this state one of super

19

learning, where you are open to all suggestion! The part of the brain that can discern (prefrontal cortex) does not start developing until our early teen years (and research suggests is not fully developed until age 25).[2] So, if you watched your parents very stressed when discussing finances or work, then you may have absorbed this style of coping and be enacting that today as an adult.

You might also know that too much stress, high levels of cortisol (the stress hormone), and lengthy timeframes of coping with high stress can impact your health. Your immune system might be taxed (perhaps you can recall suffering with a head cold or worse if you have ever felt *really* stressed), blood pressure might increase, and your susceptibility to other serious illnesses is magnified. But how can stress impact memory?

How Stress Looks		
Body Symptoms	*Emotional Symptoms*	*Behavioral Symptoms*
•stress headaches	•anxiety	•over-eating
•back pain	•restlessness	•under-eating
•chest pain	•worrying	•angry outbursts
•heart disease	•irritability	•drug or alcohol abuse
•heart palpitations	•depression	•increased smoking
•high blood pressure	•sadness	•social withdrawal
•decreased immunity	•anger	•crying spells
•stomach upset	•feeling insecure	•relationship conflicts
•sleep problems	•lack of focus	
	•burnout	
	•forgetfulness	

Stress and Memory

There has been much research done over the past two decades that indicates stress and the hormones released during and after a stressful event can actually change our learning and memory processes.[3] When stress occurs around the time of learning (think of students in a classroom here), it interferes with memory retrieval (again think of academically sound students who underperform on exams). It is a complex process, but suffice to say that a small amount of stress may help learning, but high levels impair functioning. Researchers like to present the relationship as an inverted (upside down) U-shape.[4]

Remember the stress hormone cortisol? It actually reaches a peak level of concentration approximately 20 to 30 minutes after something stressful has occurred and enters the brain to bind to two different receptors. These receptors then have a direct impact on cognition.[5] Stress affects the formation of memories and also memory retrieval. If you have ever had something highly emotional or distressing happen, you typically remember it well too. I did mention it is a complex process! It seems that severe stress during events can lock down memory formation but also interfere with accessing and processing it later on. This is why some people with conditions such as post-traumatic stress disorder find it difficult to move past those distressing memories.

Harvard University researchers also highlight that while stress affects your brain and your mood, it also promotes inflammation. This may affect your heart health and is why the common old "stress" has been associated with multiple chronic diseases of the brain and heart.[6] There is also evidence that stress can literally rewire your brain: your decision-making section (prefrontal cortex) becomes less active, and the stress center (amygdala) grows larger. This means it does not take as much stress to trigger it into action. We call it *amygdala hijack* when the stress center reacts very quickly and takes over your bodily responses. If you have a lot of stress in your life, daily even, and it never ends, think of it as exercising that muscle of the amygdala: it is getting a workout and getting stronger. The prefrontal cortex, which you actually need for good decision-making, is less active and weaker.

This is why, in the peak of a stressful moment, you may feel your mind go offline and all common sense leave you. It is very hard to think straight if you are highly stressed, let alone have a great memory!

The Fight or Flight Syndrome

Stress is the response to threats, actual or perceived. The way our bodies respond might be to get ready to fight; in other circumstances they will want to flee or run away from distress (flight). We now have other recognized ways people react. Some people freeze (become immobile during stress), and others might actually faint. Researchers also suggest some might fawn (an instinctual response associated with a need to avoid conflict and trauma and people please[7]), and others become frightened.[8] Basically, your body cannot tell the difference between the war in your emotions and mind and an actual, real war. So if you feel stressed, your endocrine glands make lots of cortisol in order to do one of the F responses. When you relax you make lots of DHEA (the cell repair hormone). Interestingly, the same precursors are used to build both DHEA and cortisol, so tapping is a way to keep the DHEA production happening!

Depression and Memory

Depression can exist outside of memory problems, and for various reasons. It is known, however, that feeling depression, or suffering depression as a clinical disorder, can affect decision-making, everyday forgetfulness, and short-term memory loss. Just like stress and anxiety, having symptoms of depression can make it harder to have your memory work for you. The types of symptoms we see in depressed people include feeling sad or hopeless, having little energy, experiencing a loss of interest in things that usually make you feel happy or good, feeling shame or guilt, having changes in your sleep (sleeping more or not enough), and losing weight or appetite. Some people also have physical issues such as pain and might have thoughts about dying. If any of these seem true for you, we do recommend you reach out to someone for professional support.

It seems that one part of the brain that is involved in memory and learning (the hippocampus) is very sensitive to stress and is smaller in people who are depressed. This area and the stress center (amygdala) are closely linked, and so high stress in someone's life can lead to more memory issues as well as lower mood. Because of the relationship here, it makes sense to target stress with tapping and then also depressive symptoms if needed. As feelings of stress calm down, and you feel more in control, you may also feel a benefit of improved mood.

The Good News

The good news is there are several things that can protect you during stress (and depression), and therefore protect your memory and functioning. Research shows that taking concrete actions to deal with stress is highly recommended, thinking in certain positive ways is beneficial, and, above all, having a really robust support system (people you can ask for support) is vital. As a first step, though, I would highly recommend tapping to calm the mind and body, as then any positive thought strategies and an increased ability to reach out to others will be easier. After all, we are all about using tapping here to cope. Tapping is highly effective for reducing anxiety, stress, and other emotional issues and works on both real and imagined stressors (e.g., children afraid of something in the dark). And we have biological evidence to show that it works. There is also research—highlighted below—that supports tapping for depression.

The Studies on Tapping and Cortisol

There have been quite a few tapping research trials that have measured biomarkers to show it positively impacts blood pressure, the immune system response, brain waves, resting heart rate, heart rate variability and heart coherence, and (of course) cortisol. I encourage you to read the paper that summarizes all the major changes,[9] but for now let's look at the two major cortisol trials.

In 2012 Dr. Dawson Church conducted a study in the United States[10] where adult participants were randomly assigned to either a tapping group who tapped for stress, a psychotherapy group who received a supportive interview about stress, or a no treatment group who read magazines. They all spent one hour in their intervention, and they were all individual sessions. Salivary cortisol samples were collected immediately before and 30 minutes after the intervention. The researchers also measured psychological distress symptoms about stress.

The tapping group showed statistically significant improvements in anxiety (decreased by 58.34 percent), depression (decreased by 49.33 percent), the overall severity of symptoms (decreased by 50.5 percent), and symptom breadth (decreased by 41.93 percent). More importantly, the tapping group experienced a significant decrease in cortisol levels (by 24.39 percent) compared with the supportive interview and magazine groups (cortisol reduced by 14.25 percent and 14.44 percent, respectively). Basically, the decrease in cortisol levels in the tapping group was mirrored with the improvement in psychological distress.

In 2019 I replicated this study in Australia[11] but made one small change: we delivered the same three interventions but did so in a group format rather than individual sessions. Everything else was exactly the same as the original study. We made this change to take advantage of an aspect unique to tapping: borrowed benefits. Borrowing benefits means that simply watching someone else do tapping on their issues, while tapping along with them, can help you reduce the emotional intensity of your own issues.[12] The probable explanation is that we all have mirror neurons and the act of watching someone else tapping activates our mirror neurons (and we feel the change is happening to us too).

The act of delivering our trial as group sessions resulted in a significant 43.6 percent reduction in cortisol over one hour. This was almost double the decrease Church's study found by administering tapping individually. The supportive interview group had a 19.5 percent decrease (very similar to the 14.25 percent from the original study), but our magazine group had an increase in their cortisol levels by two percent! Perhaps taking time out to read when you are stressed does not really do much to your cortisol! Our study also showed that tapping in groups may result in better outcomes.

Can you imagine now having the ability to physically lower your own stress hormone levels whenever the need arises? Can you also imagine your loved ones and children having this ability? Imagine having:

- better focus and concentration,
- an increased sense of calm,
- decreased stress and anxiety, fear of failure, and procrastination,
- improved impulse control,
- increased self-awareness,
- skillful responses to difficult emotions and ability to express of emotions in a self-empowered way, and
- increased empathy and understanding of others.

The Studies on Depression

Depression is an emerging area in tapping research since it can be quite complex. But the studies on university students[13] show that just four sessions of tapping for depression significantly reduced their symptoms. My own research compared tapping to a gold standard therapy (cognitive behavioral therapy, CBT),[14] and two of the four participants in the CBT group and three of the six participants in the tapping group no longer met the diagnostic criteria for major depression at the end of the eight-week program. While the CBT group did not maintain this, those in the tapping group were still reporting an absence of symptoms after six months. There are suggestions for how to use tapping for depression coming up.

Getting Started with Tapping for Stress

I highly suggest getting in the habit of daily tapping. You will not have to tap forever on every single thing that happened in your life. Research shows tapping has the ability to generalize so many things in your life. For example, if you tapped on a memory from the past where you got tongue-tied speaking in front of a group, after reaching a state of calm thinking about that memory, you may find that all the other times the same thing happened feel better also. This is the generalization effect in tapping—you may only need to tap on one or two significant times when something happened, and your feeling of calm generalizes to other similar memories when you think back.

It turns out the other research studies (some of mine included) also show that, at two-year follow-up, tapping on certain issues lasts. The issues do not return, and our participants' ability to manage them lasts (and even better—they don't really do any more tapping after our trials end!). Daily tapping for five to 10 minutes will build a habit that will have long-lasting effects. You will lower cortisol, calm yourself, develop focus, and manage all emotions differently in the future.

> Tapping daily will create space, changing impulsive reactions to thoughtful responses. Attach your daily tapping to an activity you already do. For example, brushing your teeth or having your morning brew might now be the time you also tap for five or 10 minutes.

To complete the exercises below, have a pen and paper ready.

Here are the two areas we typically tap on for stress: your stress feelings or bodily sensations and your thoughts about stress.

Always remember to be specific to your own physical sensation, selecting words to describe your situation or feelings/thoughts. Tapping works best when you are very specific.

So rather than saying "I feel stressed" when you are tapping (even though that may be a good descriptor), ask yourself where in your body you feel it.

If you are feeling stressed right now (or have recently felt this way and can think back to it) think about how it makes you feel.

If you can feel it in your body, where is that? If it is in your stomach, solar plexus area, or head, write that down.

The next questions to ask about the time you are thinking of (or right now if you currently feel stressed) are: what do you tell yourself when you feel stressed? What thoughts are in your head (e.g., I can't cope, I am overwhelmed, there is so much to do)? Write these down too.

Now write the level of intensity on the ideas above out of 10. Remember with tapping, 10 is the most distress/feeling/sensation you can have and 0 is you feel completely calm or neutral.

Now let's tap.

Feelings First

While tapping the side of the hand point (on either hand), repeat these phrases out loud and substitute or change the words in bold to fit your exact situation. Let's start with the first words you wrote down—how you feel.

"Even though I feel **completely exhausted** at the moment, I accept myself anyway."

"Even though I feel **stressed with everything I have to do**, I accept how I feel."

"Even though I feel **so overwhelmed and swamped**, I accept that this is how I feel right now."

Now for the reminder phrases. Tap through each of the points from the image in Chapter 1 or from the handout, speaking them out loud. Remember to use your exact words from your setup statements above.

Eyebrow: "I feel so tired."
Side of Eye: "I'm feeling overwhelmed."
Under Eye: "I feel swamped."
Under Nose: "I feel stressed."
Chin: "This is overwhelming."
Collarbone: "I am SO exhausted."
Under Arm: "I feel completely overwhelmed."
Head: "I feel so stressed."

See how your body feels after a few rounds. Try to identify areas that might be holding tension, emotions, or anxiety. Keep tapping until you are a 0 or a 1 out of 10 (10 being the most anxiety, and 0 being complete calm). Write down your notes to check in later.

Body Sensations

Now let's turn to any physical sensations as an example. Select one of the body sensations you wrote down and target that. Remember to change the words in bold to fit your exact situation. You might say these as your setup statements:

"Even though I feel **tight in my chest** at the moment, I accept myself anyway."

"Even though I feel **stressed and can feel it in my stomach**, I accept how I feel."

"Even though I feel **so stressed and pressure in my head**, I accept that this is how I feel right now."

And then these reminder phrases on each point:

Eyebrow: "this tightness in my chest"

Side of Eye: "this sick feeling in my stomach"

Under Eye: "this tightness in my head"

Under Nose: "this pressure in my chest"

Chin: "this stressed feeling in my stomach"

Collarbone: "this pressure in my head"

Under Arm: "this tight stomach"

Head: "this feeling in my chest and head"

Again, keep tapping a few more rounds to see what the number out of 10 becomes. If there is one area of the body that stands out, you can just say that same phrase over and over.

Thoughts About Stress

Now let's turn to any thoughts you have about stress. Select one of the thoughts you wrote down and target that. Remember to change the words in bold to fit your exact situation. You might say these as your setup statements:

"Even though I **don't think I can cope**, I accept myself anyway."

"Even though I **think stress is bad**, I accept this thought I am having."

"Even though I **can't even think straight**, I accept that this is how I feel right now."

And then these reminder phrases on each point:

Eyebrow: "I can't cope."

Side of Eye: "this belief about stress"

Under Eye: "My stress is bad."

Under Nose: "I can't think straight."

Chin: "I can't cope at all."

Collarbone: "This stress is killing me."

Under Arm: "my beliefs about stress"

Head: "this confusion in my head"

Again, keep tapping a few more rounds to see what the number out of 10 becomes.

Extra Ways to Use Tapping for Feeling Stressed

One of the best ways (teach this to your children and teens!) is to tap just to calm down in the moment. When you feel stressed, find a quiet place (I have been known to duck off to the bathroom!) and just tap on the physical sensations (e.g., headache, tightness in chest, stomach feeling) to introduce some calm. You can also simply tap and breathe (tap on each point but just say the words *breathe* or *relax* as you tap—this is to just introduce a physiological calm, rather than address any problem, like the quick action steps in Chapter 1). You may then be in a position to start tapping on what is actually happening to make you respond in that moment with a stressed feeling. Remember that tapping is most effective when you are honest about what is happening and how you feel, but sometimes you need to get the body calmer to start to do this. This is where just tapping and saying "breathe" or "relax" might be useful in the beginning. Or don't use any words at all and just tune into your breath as you tap.

Then, when you have more time and space, use tapping to explore *why* you react in certain ways when you are stressed. Think about earlier memories in your life when you may have felt stressed, in order to track the pattern of *when* it started. You may have learned your coping skills by watching others as mentioned (e.g., parents) or because you were too young when things happened and you did not have any coping skills developed yet. You can tap on younger memories with the movie technique, which is outlined at the end of this chapter, or seek the support of a skilled practitioner to assist (see resources at the end of this book).

A final way you can use tapping for stress is to include the choices method from Chapter 1. As you say your setup statement, include an ending about how you *want* things to be.

For example, instead of stating "Even though I feel so stressed right now, I accept this is how I feel," you could say "Even though I feel so stressed out right now, I am allowing calm to come into my mind and body." You will still do tapping on feeling stressed right now, but you are being clear about how you *want* to be. You are just being open to the possibility of a positive outcome.

Getting Started with Tapping for Depression

As mentioned, targeting stress can also impact feelings of low mood. As the stress feeling reduces, the connection to depressed feelings might also decrease. However, as mentioned, if you are dealing with more significant depression symptoms such as thoughts of death or you are not eating or sleeping well, I recommend you reach out to a professional to support you.

Tapping can be used to target several areas known to affect low mood and depressed symptoms. Let's look at behaviors to begin.

Have you found yourself no longer doing things you previously enjoyed? Do you have less energy than usual? If you could rate your energy levels out of 10 (10 = no energy at all, 0 = feel great), what rating would you give your energy?

Start tapping with "Even though I have no energy … I accept this is what is happening right now." Use the reminder phrase "this low energy." Re-rate your energy levels and repeat rounds until the intensity is down to a 1 or 0 or until a new feeling arises.

When you stop doing the things you used to enjoy, you may miss out on experiencing pleasant feelings and positive experiences. What are your thoughts about this? What we know is that when a depressed person experiences a lack of motivation, it may lead to cutting back on fun activities and neglecting daily tasks. It seems that the less you do, the more lethargic you feel. You begin to feel worse due to the lack of positives in your life; many people say "I'll do it when I feel better," and they are waiting to feel better before going out or taking action.

Usually when you feel physically tired, you need rest, but when you are depressed, resting more makes you feel more tired. In addition, doing nothing gives you more time to think depressing thoughts. Becoming more active, however, has several advantages: it can help you feel better, it can help you feel less tired, and it can help you think more clearly. Just a little bit of activity can give your mind something else to think about, provide a sense of achievement, and add a sense of fun.

So, if you were to think about doing more activity or even exercise in your life right now—how does this make you feel and what thoughts come to mind? Make a note of these. People may feel overwhelmed at the idea of this, or resistance, or even anger. Just see what comes up.

Let's do some tapping on the feeling you have about doing more activity.

"Even though I feel ... at the idea of doing more exercise or activity in my life to help my mood, I accept myself."

Use the reminder phrase of the feeling—e.g., overwhelmed, resisting, angry.

If you have negative thoughts about doing more activity, put those in the setup statements too.

"Even though I think ... [I won't be able to do more, I am too tired, etc.], I accept these thoughts." The reminder phrases might be the thoughts—e.g., "I just can't," "I am too tired," "it's too hard."

Keep tapping and make note of what comes up. In Chapter 6 there is a section on tapping to enjoy exercise that may be very helpful to explore.

The other main area traditional therapies target in depression is increasing pleasurable activities in life. Pleasurable experiences may lift your spirits. The ones that leave you with a sense of purpose and meaningful relationships may do even more: protect your body against ill health.

Positive psychology, a new field of research into the good life, well-being, and happiness, provides a wealth of useful information for personal development and growth. It was founded by University of Pennsylvania psychologist Martin Seligman, who wrote the book *Authentic Happiness.* Research has found that achieving happiness requires practicing a few simple disciplines ... every day.

So, if you were to think about doing things you used to enjoy or trying new things now, how do you feel about that idea? Here is a list of activities that might be fun and pleasurable for you. Feel free to add your own fun activities to the list. The main thing here is to read this list and see what feelings or thoughts come to mind as you think about doing them. You want to see if there is any resistance or negative thoughts or feelings so you have something to tap on.

Example Pleasurable Activities

1. soaking in the bathtub
2. planning my career
3. collecting things (coins, shells, etc.)
4. going on vacation
5. recycling old items
6. relaxing
7. going on a date
8. going to a movie
9. jogging, walking
10. listening to music
11. thinking I have done a full day's work
12. recalling past parties
13. buying household gadgets
14. lying in the sun
15. planning a career change
16. laughing
17. thinking about my past trips
18. listening to others
19. reading magazines or newspapers
20. hobbies (stamp collecting, model building, etc.)
21. spending an evening with good friends
22. planning a day's activities
23. meeting new people
24. remembering beautiful scenery
25. saving money
26. card and board games
27. going to the gym, doing aerobics
28. eating
29. thinking how it will be when I finish school
30. getting out of debt/paying debts

If you have looked at the list and noticed any negative feelings or thoughts, rate them out of 10 for intensity, and put them in the setup statements.

"Even though I feel ... when I look at the list and think about doing those activities, I accept that this is happening." (The reminder phrase will be the feeling words.)

"Even though I think … or tell myself … when I look at the list and think about doing those activities, I accept that this is happening." (The reminder phrase will be the thought or what you are telling yourself.)

Make a note of anything else that comes up as you are tapping, and keep checking the list to see if your interest in doing any of those things changes.

* * *

Before we finish this section, I wanted to share a story from the 2020 coronavirus pandemic. It was an incredibly stressful time for many people with lengthy lockdown periods and restrictions. This story is from tapping practitioner Kim A. Cobler, who assisted Sheila with her stress of staying at home during lockdown (this was done virtually and online due to restrictions). You will read that Sheila quickly remembers a memory and Kim uses the movie technique to process it. While these types of memories are best supported in professional settings, you will notice her stress relating to the lockdown dissipates because she taps on a leg of the table.

* * *

EFT Tapping for Coronavirus Stay-at-Home Stress

This was the first time I worked with Sheila, and it was her first exposure to tapping. We had talked about EFT before and decided that, rather than me sending her information to read, we would plan on a longer initial appointment and I would give her an overview before we started.

At the beginning of the call, we went over the basics and I let her know this was a safe nonjudgmental space to work on anything. I also made it a point to let her know that, in the case of challenging or hard topics, I had gentle techniques to guide the direction and speed we worked on things. I let her know, too, that it is important for us to use her words and thoughts, so if anything doesn't resonate for her, please speak out and correct me or if new things come up, don't hesitate to let me know.

This was the beginning of the stay-at-home order for coronavirus. There was a lot of family in Sheila's home, and she was feeling stress that she couldn't support others as she wanted. I had her focus on the stress she was feeling and where she felt it in her body. She felt it in her throat. The SUD was a 7. I asked her if an event came to mind where she might have felt that feeling in her throat before.

Sheila responded quickly with a time she had been molested as a child and the terrible feeling of being out of control and not being able to speak out. I confirmed it was a one-time event and short in duration. She didn't want to talk about it out loud, so I had her use the silent movie technique. I described what we would be doing and reassured her that I would lead her through. I had her identify a safe starting place for the movie. She gave the movie a title. At first, she wanted to make the title "I hate him." I didn't want to use such a potentially negatively charged name, so we talked about the importance of having a neutral title and changed the name to "The Game." We tapped on the title of her movie.

Once the title was a SUD of 0, I had her start from the safe place and go through the movie until she got to the first point where there was a surge of emotion. She identified the first point as "embarrassed" and said it was a 10. We tapped it down to a 1.

I had her start again from the safe place and go through the movie. She identified a point that happened before the last point, but she hadn't realized it had a charge. She named it "stupid" and we tapped it from a 7 to 0.

Sheila started from the safe place again and went through the movie until she got to a surge. This point she identified as "Not Me." We tapped on this, taking it from an 8 to a 0.

When she went through the movie again, she was able to go through the entire movie without a surge. She was so happy. She said she had been aware that she needed to do something to address this event and she felt really good.

I wanted to make sure we had taken care of the presenting issue. I had her close her eyes and go back to the stress she had been feeling and asked how her throat was feeling. She said it was down to about a 3 or a 4. I had her describe the feeling in her throat and asked if it had a color or a texture. It was blue and felt like a big round knot blocking her throat. We tapped on the stress feeling in her throat and all the aspects—the blue color and the big knot blocking her throat. It went down to a SUD of 0.

When I had her take a deep breath and think about the stress, she said it was gone. I asked her how her throat was feeling, and she said it felt great. I asked her if she thought she could speak her peace and support her family like she wanted. She was listing things she could do and ways she could speak up and let them know what she needed and still allow them to get their needs met. She had changed from being tight in her neck and facial expressions to smiling and relaxed.

She later wrote a review stating how amazing the session was and that it helped her resolve something she had struggled with for years, stating it as a huge breakthrough.

The Movie Technique

Sometimes as you are tapping, a fleeting thought passes through your mind, sometimes related, sometimes unrelated. Often this is part of your unconscious mind letting you know an earlier reason, or time in life where a decision point may have happened.

We do recommend that, if distressing memories come to mind, you engage with a professionally trained tapping practitioner to support you in processing it (see the end of the book for recommendations). This is the process they may use:

1. Imagine the movie or memory and give it a title. Make it something fairly neutral such as "The Day That Thing Happened." This allows you to have some distance if it is distressing. Give the movie title a rating out of 10 (10 = most distress and 0 = complete calm or neutral). Tap just for the SUDS for the movie title until it feels low in intensity before moving to step two.

2. Now imagine the memory on a movie screen and you are watching it from the seats or even the projection box in a movie theater—so you are watching yourself in the movie at a younger age. Start the movie memory at a neutral point in time, before anything happened. At no point are you in the movie yourself—you are always watching it from a distance.

3. Play the movie memory very slowly from the neutral point, and stop the movie every time a negative feeling, belief, or anything else comes up (rate that one section with a SUDS out of 10). It could be a body sensation too.

4. Tap for that one little section of the movie until it feels calmer in the SUDS rating you gave it, then rewind the movie memory and play it again to see if that section has cleared in intensity. Stop at the next increase in intensity and do the same—rate it and tap on those aspects you notice.

5. Keep doing this until each rewind results in a neutral movie by the end.

This process does not change that the memory happened to you, but it does release any emotional charge that still might be in there.

Quick Action Steps

1. Put this into practice today. Find some quiet time (even 10 minutes is enough) and tap on something that is still bothering you

from last week. See how you feel in emotion and also in your body, as well as any thoughts you might be thinking about that event.

2. Make some notes about your memory belief from the quick action steps in Chapter 1 (*I believe I have a ... memory*). If you wrote words/phrases such as *poor, bad, like a sieve,* write down at least three times in life where this belief has been confirmed (i.e., something happened and you felt you did have this type of memory).

The next chapter takes a closer look at how tapping can be used for everyday memory issues. If you want to remember why you walked into that room, or where you put the keys, or even someone's name, then this is the chapter to assist with that. Reducing stress generally is a good thing, but using tapping in this way can have a profound impact on how your memory functions. There are plenty of stories coming up from real people, so let's head there now.

CHAPTER 3

Tapping for Everyday Memory Issues

I can't blame my short-term memory lapses on my age, says tapping practitioner Robert Dickson. *I've had this problem all my life. Neurofeedback sessions have helped a lot, but there are still gaps that leave me frustrated and even exasperated at times. To try to fill these gaps, I've developed some habits that help, like putting my billfold, glasses, car keys, etc., in the same location every night when I empty my pockets, so that finding them in the morning will be routine.*

Recently, I was rushing around getting ready to leave for work, when I realized my billfold was not in its usual place. Immediately, my anxiety rose, triggering thoughts such as, what if I get stopped by a traffic cop on the way to work? What will I do if I have to make a credit card purchase?

I frantically raced through the house, revisiting all the places I had been last night: the living room, my home office, my wife's computer desk, my clothes closet, the kitchen and dinette. In my closet, I'd twice checked the coat and pants pockets of the clothes I had been wearing yesterday. When the second time around the house didn't locate the billfold, I found my anxiety enhanced by frustration. The thought of having to notify the credit card companies to cancel and reissue, as well as having to apply for a replacement driver's license, added anger to the above emotions.

Then a thought popped into my mind: Why not try tapping? Though new to this tool, with still a lot to learn, I sat down and began tapping:

Even though I know I've been careless with my billfold, I very much would like to remember where it is, and I'm a very worthwhile person.

I repeated this several times. Suddenly, the closet flashed into my mind. I rejected the image at first, because I had already twice gone through the pockets of the suit I had worn. Then I got another flash. I hadn't worn the suit, only the coat. I'd worn a pair of different colored slacks!

Rushing to the closet, I pulled out the slacks I'd worn. There in a pocket was my billfold! Plus, I still had time to get to work by opening hour.

While this may seem a trivial thing to get upset about, my first emotional reaction had the potential to set my whole day on the wrong track. Tapping relieved my anxiety, frustration, and anger, and allowed my short-term memory circuits to do their job.

* * *

I am sure everyone reading the above story can relate! Who hasn't misplaced glasses, keys, the remote for the television, or even something really important? I lost the Elf on the Shelf many years ago when our girls were young and only realized just before December 1, when the Elf was due to "appear" on his trip from Santa! (Elf on the Shelf is a Christmas tradition where a special elf arrives from the North Pole to encourage children to behave themselves. Santa's helper elf watches the children by day, and each night it returns to the North Pole to report on whether they were naughty or nice.) I ripped the bedroom cupboard apart looking for where I had hidden the elf 12 months before. Alas, I had no luck. I desperately had another shipped through eBay to get here on time to avoid the girls thinking the elf never came back because they were naughty! I did forget to tap! I found the first elf months later (in a sleeping bag—what was I thinking!?), and in the following years two elves turned up. Hilarious in hindsight, but I wish I had remembered to tap *to remember*!

* * *

EFT trainer and advanced practitioner Naomi Janzen shares her own personal experience of remembering to tap for the everyday things.

I was standing in the fifth or sixth shop I had to dash into during a day full of errands. As I waited for the sales person to finish with another customer, I realized I had no idea why I was in that store. I hadn't written it down anywhere, and it was a store I'd never been in before. I knew what I needed to get was here ... but could not for the life of me remember what it was. Then I remembered a past client who has

used tapping for memory, and heard my own advice: "Give it a try."
So, I stepped away to a part of the store where I was a bit out of sight
and started tapping, mouthing silently, "Even though I know I had to
get something in this store but I can't remember what...." In the mid-
dle of the second round, it came to me. There was a particular stuffed
toy with an unusual name that a friend had said was sold here and
was the ideal baby gift! I was halfway there. Encouraged, I continued,
"Even though I know it was a stuffed toy for Suzanne's new baby but
I can't remember what it was called...." Halfway through the second
round, yet again, it came to me. Jellycat rabbit.

A year later, I was with friends at their house having an art
afternoon and we were listening to the usual instrumental movie
soundtracks when one of them announced that they were tired of the
same ones over and over and asked, "Who's got something new we can
listen to?" I remembered being in that shop where I bought the Jelly-
cat and noticing how much I liked the store music that was playing as I
went through the checkout process. I had thought of our art afternoons
and decided this would be a good music option. The woman in the shop
had told me what it was—but I had forgotten! This time I wasn't shy
about tapping in front of others. "Even though that music playing in the
shop where I got the Jellycat for Suzanne's baby was perfect for here but
I can't remember...." My friends watched, bemused. No more than two
rounds in, I had half of the answer. "It's a TV show," I announced, con-
fidently. The chuckles died out as they watched me, fascinated. "Even
though I can't remember the name of the TV show that soundtrack was
from...." Halfway through the second round, "Downton Abbey." They
stared as I located it on Spotify, hit play, and went on with my art as if
nothing had happened.

***

Tapping for the Lost Things

This chapter is all about how to use tapping to recall where you
may have left something, why you walked into a room, and maybe
even someone's name. The same principle applies: you need to tap on
what is happening right now in the moment. Like Robert's story, if you
are feeling flustered, stressed, overwhelmed, or angry with yourself,

then that's what you need to tap on. But I have some other tricks here to share.

If you have misplaced something at home, first ask yourself how you feel about this. Rate that feeling out of 10 and tap on that first. Sometimes doing this type of tapping is good to do quietly inside your own mind rather than out loud. When you tap silently repeating your reminder phrases, your mind might wander a little. This is when you might actually recall where you left something, or have a flash like Robert of clothing, furniture, or a room. This happens because the amygdala (stress center) lives next door to your memory center in your brain (the hippocampus). As the amygdala becomes quieter, the hippocampus is able to be heard and often gives you memories or thoughts about the origins of what you are tapping on.

In Chapter 2 I outlined what to do if you are tapping and a fleeting thought comes to mind (the movie technique). What is really important is to not ignore these fleeting thoughts—they are clues!

So, your tapping might start like this: "Even though I can't believe I have lost that necklace and I can't remember where it is, I accept these feelings" (the reminder phrase might be "I can't believe it" or "I can't remember"). It is important to also ask yourself how you feel about losing the necklace. If you feel angry, you could tweak the setup statement to: "Even though I feel angry I have lost that necklace, how could I be so stupid, I accept this feeling" (the reminder phrase could be "so angry at myself").

The aim here is to reduce those feelings and reach a place of calm.

If during your tapping you don't have any other flashes or thoughts arise about where the item is, you could tap with this type of phrase (once you are calm): "Even though I have lost that necklace, I am staying open to remembering where I left it." In this case (because you are calm) you can engage in more positive tapping and tap the reminder phrases as "I am open to remembering." You can stop whenever you want and go about your day or week and then see what happens or whether any ideas come to mind.

What Am I Doing Here?

Have you walked into a room or cupboard and stood there wondering *why* you are there? I promised I would share what I do! I stay

39

in the room and start tapping with this exact phrase: "Even though I can't remember why I am here, I am open to remembering" (my reminder phrase is "I can't remember"). I just stand there and keep tapping with the statement that I can't remember. I don't usually have to tap for very long before it pops back in! Sometimes I tap on the face points only and that is enough. This is exactly what we teach students to say in exams, too: when they cannot remember an answer to something they know they have studied, we get them to tap and say "I can't remember" silently to themselves. We do also teach them to tap discreetly so no one notices in the exam (more in the next chapter on this!).

If you identify as someone who generally is a forgetful person, even for the little daily things, you could also try tapping on this. I always like to ask this type of question: What do you think of people who have amazing memories? If you were to think about someone in your life who *does* have a great memory, what do you think of them?

Just say you were to think of your Aunt Ruth, who always remembers people's names, her shopping list, and even her nursery school teacher's name. You may think to yourself, "Wow! She is amazing. I could never remember things like she does." In this case, you might compare yourself to her and feel inferior, worse at memory than she, or even hopeless.

These are the feelings and thoughts you can tap on.

It is entirely possible you could think of Aunt Ruth and think that it would be exhausting to try to remember all of those things every day. I don't have time or the mental strength to do that. So instead of thinking she is amazing and wondrous with her memory, you may think it takes too much mental energy and it's not worth it. Again, these are the things you could tap on.

Here are some ideas for both angles. Read these statements out loud to see which ones seem to resonate with you more, then rate your own level of belief, feeling or thoughts about someone in your own life who has a great memory, and begin tapping.

- "Even though when I think of ... who has an amazing memory, I don't think I could ever be like that, I accept that I feel this way." (The reminder phrase might be "I can't ever be like them.")
- "Even though when I think of ... who has an amazing memory,

40

I feel inferior to them, I accept that I feel this way." (The reminder phrase might be "I feel inferior.")
- "Even though when I think of ... who has an amazing memory, I feel overwhelmed, I accept that I feel this way." (The reminder phrase might be "I feel overwhelmed.")
- "Even though when I think of ... who has an amazing memory, I feel hopeless, I accept that I feel this way." (The reminder phrase might be "I feel hopeless.")
- "Even though when I think of ... who has an amazing memory, I think that would be exhausting, I accept that I feel this way." (The reminder phrase might be "it would be exhausting.")
- "Even though when I think of ... who has an amazing memory, I don't think it is worth the effort, I accept that I feel this way." (The reminder phrase might be "not worth the effort.")

Keep your own notes as you work through these ideas. It is an excellent idea to read back in a week or two's time to see what you think then. Often the changes can be subtle, and it is not until you look back that you realize you don't believe that statement as much or no longer feel that way.

Let's have a specific look at what we believe about our memory.

* * *

My own husband is pretty awful at remembering people's names. He remembers everything about people, but not their names! I cannot tell you the number of times we have met people and he doesn't introduce me on purpose because of this memory lapse. When I question how he can recall other facts about them except their name, he has a strong belief: "I don't have a good memory for names."

This is so common: the beliefs we hold about ourselves become ingrained and our truth. When we have a strong belief, we actually look for evidence in the world to confirm it for us (we call this confirmation bias). The reason it is a bias is that there will be plenty of evidence for the opposite of your belief, but you are only looking for and tuned into the evidence that supports you. Another example might be the strong belief *all the good men are taken* (this came from one of my clients). I inquired how she could possibly know this. Had she met every man in the world? Any evidence I offered to the contrary was ignored as she had plenty of evidence that it was true: every man she met or dated did not turn out to be a "good" one, and all the men she met in committed relationships were (and therefore unavailable). Anytime a belief appears to be a sweeping generalization (I'm always late! Money is hard to come by! I'm terrible at organization!), then you know it might be one with confirmation bias attached.

Back to the name game. So, if you have a belief that you are terrible at remembering names, guess what happens when you meet someone? In the back of your mind you are whispering to yourself: "I will never remember this person's name again, I never remember names, I am hopeless at names...." Your brain does not know any better, so it complies and makes this your truth. Even memory tricks probably don't work for you. You don't remember names, remember?

Let's see how tapping can help with beliefs. While this section is about beliefs about names, you can apply the same strategy to any belief (e.g., you might be thinking of other beliefs you have now that you want to change!). We are going to examine three areas to tap on to have a perfect memory for names.

First, have some paper handy to write. Draw three columns. Write at the top of the page your belief about remembering people's names. Is it that you believe you just have a poor memory for names? Is it slightly different?

In one column write "Validity of Cognition" (this is the truth of how much you believe this is true for you). If you were to rate your belief about how poor your memory is for names, what would that be? Ten would be the most belief and 0 would represent that you don't believe this about yourself at all (the aim is to get this strength of belief down to a 0 so you don't believe this about yourself).

Start your tapping with addressing how strong this belief is for you: "Even though I truly believe I have a poor memory for remembering names, I accept myself anyway." Your reminder phrase might be "I truly believe this."

Just tap with your reminder phrase with as many rounds as you like, and regularly check in to see what the number seems to be out of 10. It might be that you just seem to *guess* the number is lowering (that you don't believe this as much) or you might hear an inner voice in your head saying something of the opposite: "I do have a good memory!"

My husband has a work colleague who actually remembers everyone's names, their children's names, and other significant people in that person's life. It is quite incredible, and makes people feel very special. I asked him how he does this, and whether he uses any specific strategies or techniques. He said he doesn't. He just decided many years ago that he thought it was an important thing to remember (as names are important to people), and he now tells himself, "I easily remember everyone's names." I laughed—it is just a belief. And the evidence he looks for is that he actually does remember names (and he does!).

The second area to tap on for having a great memory for names is for any doubt you might have that you *could* have a great memory for names. In the next column on your page, write the word "Doubt."

Say this statement out loud and listen for any chatter inside your mind that this can't come true: "I have a perfect memory for other people's names and always remember them." Say it several times out loud and pause and listen inside your mind. Do you have any chatter (thoughts) telling you that this is fiction?

Rate the level of doubt you may have about having this perfect memory out of 10 (10 = most doubt and 0 = no doubt at all) on your paper and write down the chatter that says you can't have a perfect memory. We call these *tailenders* in tapping—they are like the "yes, but" part of our brain that tell us why things aren't true for us. Here is a list of someone's tailenders from that statement above. See if any of these ring true for you.

- I have a perfect memory for other people's names and always remember them. *No you don't! Who do you think you are?*
- I have a perfect memory for other people's names and always remember them. *As if. You never remember people's names, like ever.*
- I have a perfect memory for other people's names and always remember them. *Good one! Our whole family is terrible at remembering people's names.*
- I have a perfect memory for other people's names and always remember them. *Not when you're tired you don't.*
- I have a perfect memory for other people's names and always remember them. *This is so not me! That is too much hard work.*

The ideas that come to mind when you say out loud the way you want to be (e.g., have a great memory for names) give us the very thing to tap on. Remember that tapping is all about what is true for us—so we want to tap on those tailenders to reduce the strength of belief in them (and their hold over us).

You might tap like this: "Even though I have so much doubt I will ever have a great memory for names because my whole family is terrible at this, I accept this is how I feel." The reminder phrases might be "My family taught me this" (or "I am copying my family"). The idea is to still loosen the grip of that old belief (and doubt). You can keep checking the level of your doubt as you tap through all the ideas that came to mind when you said the statement out loud.

The third area is to do tapping in the moment you run into someone and cannot recall their name. To do this you will need to do some discreet tapping (unless you are quite happy to have them ask you what you are doing tapping on your face!). This next section is one discreet way to tap in public (there is another in the next chapter).

This version of tapping uses finger points. While we may not use them anymore in clinical trials, they are very useful if you need to be discreet. Alongside each nail bed where your fingernail touches the skin is an acupressure point (see Figure 3A). You could tap on one side of this under a table (e.g., in an exam or standing in front of someone) or squeeze each side of each finger/nail bed discreetly instead. You can also still include the side of the hand point. Do both hands: they could be sitting in your lap and no one will notice. Still say the setup statement in your mind and reminder phrase as you squeeze. In this case you might be internally saying "can't remember their name," or "I'm open to recalling their name!"

Usually it will pop back in! (I still highly recommend tapping on the name issue with the first two ideas as well.) Interestingly, if you bite your nails, you are getting the same stress reduction tapping gives (you are biting the acupoint and will still feel tension release). It is better to tap though!

This discreet method is also very useful if you wake in the night and cannot get back to sleep. Instead of tapping and moving your arms, try the discreet way with your fingernails. Remember to still say what the problem is: "I can't get to sleep, my mind is racing, my back hurts."

To end this type of tapping, it is always good to conclude with positive or choices tapping. How do you want your everyday memory to be? What would you be open to?

Here are some examples of how to tap with this.

Setup statements:

- "Even though I have been forgetful in the past, I choose to realize that I have a great memory."
- "Even though I've been bringing it on myself, I choose to quickly turn this around."
- "Even though I've been focusing on

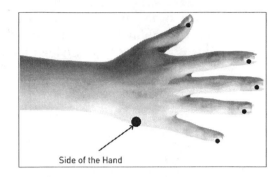

Side of the Hand

Figure 3A. Discreet tapping points along side of fingernails

having a bad memory, I choose to focus on having the most perfect, brilliant memory."

Now tap a round using positive or choice reminder phrases. You can say the same single phrase on each point if it resonates more, or different ones like those below if they are all related.

Eyebrow: "I choose to have a great memory."
Side of the Eye: "open to easily recalling names"
Under the Eye: "I am in charge of my memory."
Under Nose: "I could have a brilliant memory."
Chin: "I choose the memory I want."
Collarbone: "I can turn this around."
Under Arm: "I might enjoy this."
Top of Head: "I can tap whenever I need to for my memory."
Tap this next round with some enthusiasm!
Eyebrow: "What if it was really easy to change?"
Side of Eye: "What if I could have a perfect memory for names?"
Under Eye: "Imagine if I had a fantastic memory."
Under Nose: "Could this be possible?"
Chin: "How good would that be?!"
Collarbone: "I am open to this!"
Under Arm: "I welcome my perfect memory!"
Top of Head: "I am open to this being my reality from now on."
Of course, if tapping on any of these positive statements brings up some tailenders for you, you need to go back and tap on those. Only use the positive tapping to complete the process when you have

tapped on the other issues. Usually if you are too enthusiastic and jump to positive tapping too soon, your mind will be loud with opposition! Remember the garbage analogy from Chapter 1.

Before we finish, I want to share a story from one of my own clients who successfully used tapping for everyday forgetfulness.

* * *

Judith was in her early fifties and starting to worry about her memory. She had noticed little things such as forgetting why she was walking into a room to get something (what was it?), and even the type of word to say in a sentence (e.g., she knew she wanted to say "bottle" but couldn't remember it in the moment). She would find a replacement word to finish the sentence, but it did worry her! There wasn't any family history of dementia or serious memory disorders so she wasn't sure why it was happening.

It turned out Judith had a busy life and possibly didn't acknowledge the stress that was present. She was a parent of three young teens who all had busy lives she needed to coordinate. She had a busy full-time job as the manager of a medical practice. Also, her husband was studying for a degree while working, and she was supporting that at home too. She was coping well (she regularly went to yoga and had a strong social system of girlfriends); she used to word "busy" rather than "stressed" to describe her life.

After acknowledging that perhaps she did feel stressed with everything in her life, as well as busy, she was able to break down exactly what caused her stress. Her tapping in sessions was targeted at these three main beliefs and feelings:

- *Felt stressed not getting enough time on her own (which she often craved)*
- *Felt stressed when the house wasn't clean because of everyone's busy schedules and she found herself cleaning at midnight*
- *Felt stressed when date night with her husband was often pushed aside because of other priorities—her stress was that they were not connecting like they used to*

Each of these was tapped on, as were associated ideas that came to mind. For example, the cleaning of the house at midnight was more about worrying that people might think she was a "bad" mother for working fulltime and not fulfilling the role of a "good" mother and wife.

This was a family belief, and tapping was used to process the feelings of guilt and shame she had. After several sessions working through these, Judith started to notice she felt calmer and was coping better than before (and she thought she was coping before!). Within the next few months, she also noticed her memory had improved: she was retaining information and recalling people's names with ease, and when talking she didn't forget any words she wanted to say. She didn't directly tap on any of those issues; she only tapped on what was causing her stress.

* * *

Quick Action Steps

1. Have you lost an item (that you have never found)? Write down when it happened and how you felt about it then and also how you feel about it now. Rate those feelings out of 10 for intensity and take five minutes to tap on them one by one.
2. Next time you meet someone and hear their name for the first time, say their name back to them in greeting and tap on your fingernail points at the same time (behind your back if you like!).

The next chapter is for all the students out there! I dive deep into how tapping can be used for supercharged learning. If you have anyone studying in your house (or doing exams) or you just want to retain more of what you read when you do, this chapter will be of great use. I also show you another discreet way to tap in public places. Let's go.

CHAPTER 4

Tapping for Supercharged Learning

The usefulness of tapping in the learning or education process is simply outstanding. Tapping can be used to keep students calm while they try to learn new concepts, to limit beliefs (e.g., I can't do this!), to facilitate recall of information while in an exam, to calm down before a speech or talk, to improve grades, or to learn a new language! Because tapping has a profound effect on the stress center in the brain and can reduce the stress hormone in the brain, the flow-on effect to the prefrontal cortex (the decision-making area) means students can make clearer and more focused decisions after tapping.

Tapping for Beliefs About Learning

Sometimes, when children are just starting out in their schooling, they may develop beliefs about their ability to learn. The negative and less helpful types of these can stay with them for life! They might include:

- I'm no good at this.
- This is too hard.
- I can't spell.
- I can't do math.
- I would rather go and do....
- I can't read these words.
- I can't remember.
- I don't know how to do this.
- My brother/sister is better than me at....

Sometimes situations happen in a classroom where a teacher may make a remark that stays with a student for years or fellow students react in a negative way. For example, a teacher may remark that boys are better at spatial reasoning and complex mathematical equations (this is not true!), and a female student hears this and gives up in that moment, because the teacher said so. Another student may present their speech and stumble due to nerves. If the class snickers at them, they might decide in that moment that they are hopeless at speeches and not good enough. This can stay with them for life.

Tapping can be used to assist a child still in these early school years, a teen, or even an adult looking back agreeing that this is what they felt. If you ever feel you need the support of an EFT practitioner to assist with childhood memories from long ago, reach out for a recommendation in your area. For now, here are ways you can support someone in your own life who is in the education system and even for yourself if you are studying or learning something new.

Tapping for Learning Something New

If you start something new, how do you feel? Excited? Nervous? Eager? Worried? Whatever the feelings, you can tap on these. If you have a child learning something new (a new module in mathematics, a science topic, reading lists and spelling), ask them how they feel. This is often better done before they start their new work. For any feeling word that is more negative (*worried, scared, stressed*), ask them if they feel it anywhere specific in their body. Then, depending on age, ask them to rate the intensity out of 10 and use a setup statement like this:

"Even though I feel really stressed about this topic, and I can feel it in my [body area], I accept that this is how I feel."

Use a reminder phrase from the statement such as "stressed" and keep tapping until it no longer feels as intense or true. Then ask your child how they feel now. See if they approach their work in a calmer manner. Younger children may not need to rate out of 10 as we use a simplified version for them. Adjustments are discussed next.

If you notice that a child or teen has negative self-beliefs or statements they say about learning (e.g., this is too hard, I can't do it, math doesn't come naturally to me), you can apply tapping as discussed in Chapter 3. This is where you rate the level of belief (10 being the strongest) and tap until the belief doesn't feel true anymore. A student may have many beliefs, so target one at a time. If there is a memory of a time when the belief was formed (e.g., the teacher who humiliated them in math class when they got the answer wrong), then using tapping with the movie technique is the best option. This can also be supported by seeing a qualified practitioner.

For further reading on using tapping for teens for other issues, I recommend reading *EFT for Teens* (published by Hay House). I wrote this especially for teens to read other stories of peers who have had success with tapping for common issues (e.g., sibling issues, bullying, family issues such as divorce, and so on).

Tapping for Younger Children

Children under the age of 10 years don't tend to have so many layers to their issues, and they often don't need the movie technique. They usually just need to tap on the exact feeling they are having in the moment, and it collapses quickly. They also often feel sensations in their body fairly easily, and you can focus there. We tend to use only four acupoints for children under 10 years (then the standard eight acupoints for older teens). It is recommended they use both hands, and if you have a puppet of a bear with the acupoints on it, this will make it even more enjoyable to tap!

In addition to using the child's exact words for the problem part of the setup statement, you also need to use an ending that feels relevant to the child. Here are some variations that children can use for the setup statement:

- "Even though I have this problem [insert actual words], I still like myself."
- "Even though I have this problem [insert actual words], I can forgive myself for this."
- "Even though I have this problem [insert actual words], I want to change this today."
- "Even though I have this problem [insert actual words], I want to let this go."
- "Even though I have this problem [insert actual words], I will be OK."
- "Even though I have this problem [insert actual words], I am OK."

- "Even though I have this problem [insert actual words], my mom/dad/pet/teacher still likes (or loves) me."

Begin by saying: "The first step is to think about your problem." If the child is already upset you can skip this part, as it is obvious the child is thinking about the issue or feeling.) Then say something like: "This exercise will calm you down and help you feel better. If you learn this exercise you can be upset only when *you* choose to be upset." If a child is very young (four or five years old) you could just say, "There are some magic spots on our face and chest, and when we tap on them, we feel better. Would you like to give that a go to feel better right now?"

Next say: "Now we want to know how upset you are." For younger children use out-stretched arms (this would equal a 10) to measure how upset the child is. Use hands with palms touching to indicate no upset (this would equal 0). Older children may have no problem with telling you on a 0-to-10 scale how upset they are.

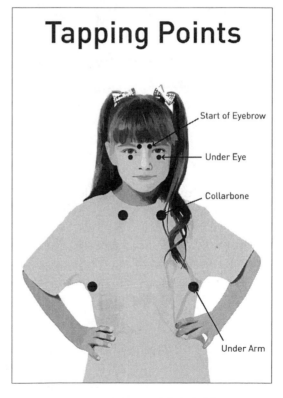

Now say: "OK, the first step is to tap the side of your hand." Using your hand as an example, show them how to tap on the fleshy side of the hand. You can tell the child it is called the side-of-the-hand spot. This spot can also be introduced as the friendly spot since that is where you touch another person's hand when you shake hands to show you are "friendly."

Figure 4A. Tapping points for children under 10 years

Use a setup statement such as: "Even though I have this problem, I am a super kid."

Then the four acupoints we use are in Figure 4A and described here:

- First "tapping" point: use three or four fingers and tap between the eyebrows.
- Second point: use two fingers from each hand and tap on the bony part under each eye.
- Third point: use a closed fist on the chest just below the collarbone (like Tarzan).
- Fourth point: tap under both arms. This is like giving yourself a hug. Wrap your arms around your body and pat under both arms about a palm's width below the armpit. For younger children you can call this the "monkey spot" and have them tap with each hand under the same arm. They get a kick out of this!

Extra Ideas for Tapping with Younger Children

Tapping can be applied during the learning process. Some beliefs were highlighted above, and these can be directly targeted before or after school activities.

For example, a child may come home and say, "Today we had a test, and it was so hard!"

You can tap directly on "Even though the test was so hard today and I felt … my teacher still likes me." You could ask them how they felt about the test, or what they think will happen next. Tapping can be used to target future worries: they may think they will fail the test or receive a certain poor score. Even though this hasn't happened yet, tapping can be used to reduce the worry.

A child may be learning spelling words or times tables and find it difficult to easily remember. You can make it a game to tap while you work with your child, to spell the words out as you tap, or tap on any/all of the points when they are trying to recall the correct spelling. This action itself will keep the body and brain calm so they can more easily access their memory center. We know it is the actual tapping on the acupuncture points that sends a calming signal to the stress center in the brain, so tapping whenever you feel stressed (even without words) will help.

As mentioned, tapping with bears or puppets can be fun for children too. They can tap on the same acupoint on the bear and then their own face/body and "teach" the bear their spelling words too. Creativity is key here! When my youngest daughter was about seven years old, I asked her how she would tell a friend about tapping and what it was. She had grown up with tapping, so it was "normal" for her. She said: "I'd just tell them there are magic spots on your face and body and if you tap on them, you feel happier." Asking a child their ideas often gives us a way to share it with others, and in a way they will accept and embrace.

That daughter of ours is now 15 years old and still taps. She sometimes asks me to help her friends!

I tapped with a seven-year-old child, Bailey, some years ago on a situation where a spelling test had not gone well. I didn't know that this was the story at the time; Bailey's mother had reached out just saying that Bailey had been doing well at school and suddenly wasn't. I knew if it was sudden then something must have happened.

I started by just asking generally how school was going. Bailey made a face and poked his tongue out, which I took to mean "yuck." I asked what his favorite subjects were, and he said "recess" (clearly play time). It used to be writing, he added, but not anymore. I asked him how he felt about that, but he just shrugged his shoulders. I showed him my Tapping Bear (I have several in my room) and said the bear needed a name. Would he name my bear? He called him Jimbo.

I said Jimbo had magic spots and if you tap with two fingers on them they make Jimbo feel better. Bailey tried this with the bear and thought it was pretty good. I then said we have the same magic spots on us (we tapped on Jimbo's and then our own together) and that when we tap on them, we can feel better too! He seemed to be engaged at this point and curious.

Now Bailey's mom was sitting in the corner of the room as this was a young child, and she was pretty surprised at how engaged Bailey was because he didn't actually want to come and see me!

I said, "I wonder how Jimbo would feel if he used to like writing but now he didn't." Bailey said Jimbo would feel sad. This was my cue to show on the bear how to tap for feeling sad. Bailey helped me tap on Jimbo's points saying he felt sad, and after a few rounds I asked if he had ever felt sad about writing. Bailey nodded, and I suggested that he could tap on that too, and so we did for a few rounds. His mom tapped along in the corner of the room.

I wasn't using the SUDS system of numbers here, just asking Bailey if he felt better, different, or otherwise. He said he felt lighter in his chest area after a few rounds of tapping on sadness. I then asked when he stopped liking writing, and he immediately offered, "When I didn't get the spelling words right." I asked if he wanted to tap on that day (I didn't even know when it was but I guessed it was around the time his ability at school declined), and he started tapping before I even finished asking!

We tapped: "Even though that test was so hard, and I couldn't write all the words in time, I'm a good friend!"

We were pretty simplistic in our words and focused on the test being "so hard" and that there "wasn't enough time," as these were the most important things to Bailey. We tapped for about four rounds, and Bailey started to visibly relax. He started playing with the bear by then and stopped tapping, so we ended the session. I told Bailey and his mom they could tap with a Pixar style video I had created whenever he wanted to feel better ("Ellie the Tapping Buddy"— available on my YouTube channel) and he could get his own bear too. I also showed him how he could tap on his fingernails in the tests (under the desk) if he felt nervous or couldn't remember the words.

I checked in with his mom the next week and asked how Bailey was with school. She said he came home the day after our session very excited with his homework sheet. He had done another spelling test, completed it in time, and achieved 80 percent correct. He said he tapped under the table just once—and showed his best friend how to tap too! Over the following school term, he re-engaged in his work and his grades remained stable and back to his ability level.

* * *

Part of why I love working with younger children is they rarely complicate the process and just get on with the tapping—because they feel better afterwards! Bailey was a wonderful example of a child who had a negative experience and was able to overcome it instead of making it part of his education story.

Teens and older students may be not so easy, but there are other ways to engage them. Let's look now.

Extra Ideas for Tapping with Older Children

Teens often like the idea of including choice in their setup statements. Dr. Patricia Carrington pioneered the "I choose" statements, adding the words "I choose" to the end of the setup statement. For example:

- "Even though I couldn't remember the answers on the test, I choose to be ok."
- "Even though I feel angry at my teacher, I choose to be calm when I am doing my school work."
- "Even though I'm nervous about giving that talk on Tuesday, I choose to be calm and confident."

Most people only tap when they feel a negative feeling. But you can use tapping for positive statements. It is highly recommended you only do this *after* you have reduced any negative feelings associated with a memory, thought, or feeling. You can then do some rounds of positive tapping to instill any new feeling or belief you would like to have. For instance:

- "Even though I was really nervous about giving that talk next week, I now feel calm and confident." (You can use "calm and confident" as the reminder phrase.)
- "Even though I couldn't remember that person's name, I now feel clear and focused." (The reminder phrase is "clear and focused.")

Tapping for Tests and Exams

It is rare to find someone who loves exams. (This is my belief, at least!) Many students feel very stressed, and we know stress robs the brain of logical thought processes and the ability to think clearly. Tapping helps calm that down and enables the memory center to recall what was studied. The minute someone is stressed or nervous in an exam or during a speech, it is actually really hard to recall what you learned or the next part of the presentation!

Some of our clinical trial research was in secondary schools where we taught the students how to use tapping for test situations (you can access the research outcomes over on the webpage for this book). The types of things they tapped on were statements such as:

55

- "I won't remember the answers."
- "I might fail."
- "What if I disappoint my parents?"
- "I hate exams."
- "I feel so nervous in exams."
- "What if my mind goes blank?"

We used all of these ideas in setup statements exactly as the students said them. We have taught teachers how to use tapping before a test in class, so the students stay calmer, and then after it is over in case anyone still has worry about how they performed. They often report an improvement in grades when they use tapping like this! In this next story Margaret Loudon, a tapping practitioner, went into a school to help the students with their anxiety about exams. The story also includes what the students thought and how it affected them.

* * *

A practitioner we know asked a class to think about their upcoming SATs and how they all felt on a scale of 0 to 10, where 0 is no anxiety and 10 is the most extreme anxiety. The majority of students had anxiety levels of between 5 and 7. She showed them how to tap using all the points, and they said "Even though I'm a bit worried about the SATs, I'll be okay."

After the first round of tapping, the numbers of students and the anxiety level difference was:

1 remained the same
1 dropped 1 point (out of 10)
19 dropped 3–5 points
2 dropped 7 points

They kept tapping: "Even though I might get the answers wrong, I'm still okay." After this round one student said, "I'm not worried about getting the answers wrong. I'm worried about reading the question wrong." She explained that she often gives the incorrect answer because of this when in fact she knows the right answer.

So, they said, "Even though I'm worried about reading the question wrong, I'm still okay" and "Even though I might not have enough time, I'm still OK." After this, 21 students reported they were down to 0 or less than 0.

The Wednesday after the SATs, the practitioner returned to

the school to find out how the students had coped with the tests. The
teacher reported that they were totally relaxed from the moment they
entered the classroom on the Monday morning.

What the students said:

- *"I was very worried about the SATs, but they were the easiest thing I've ever done in my life."*
- *"The tapping helped me drastically. It kept me calm for the SATs."*
- *"My SATs were good. Tapping made them easy."*
- *"I expected them to be harder, but they were easier."*
- *"I felt really calm after being so worried."*

* * *

The main ways to use tapping for exams include while studying and on any negative beliefs you have about exams and also during the exams.

Tapping While Studying

Students can tap on those beliefs above if they feel stuck, frustrated they can't understand a concept, or are finding it hard to remember. These will all be beliefs. For example: "Even though I feel so frustrated I can't get this, I'll be ok." The reminder phrase will be "frustrated."

It is also good to remind them to use tapping for their beliefs about having a great memory for exams. A reminder of some phrases: "Even though I can't always easily remember what I learn, I am open to the possibility of this." The reminder phrase might be "it's not easy for me." After tapping through to reduce the intensity of this belief, try tapping with some positive phrases (note: this is only recommended after reducing their negative beliefs). "Even though I have struggled with remembering in the past, I can easily remember anything from now on."

The reminder phrases may be:
Eyebrow: "I've got an unlimited capacity for remembering."
Side of Eye: "I amaze myself with my capacity for remembering."
Under Eye: "I have an absolutely brilliant memory."
Under Nose: "My memory improves every day."

Chin: "Every day, in every way my memory improves."
Collarbone: "I have an absolutely brilliant memory."
Under Arm: "My memory is brilliant."
Top of Head: "My memory is absolutely brilliant."

Tapping During the Exam

Using the discreet fingernail points from Chapter 3, students can tap while in the exam room with their hands in their lap. They just need to silently say what they are worrying about and squeeze their fingernail beds. For example: "Even though I can't remember what ... I choose to stay calm right now." The reminder phrase would be "can't remember."

The university students I teach tell me that this never fails them. They just keep repeating "I can't remember," becoming calmer as they do, and eventually the answer will pop into their mind. I do tell them this only works if they have studied the information!

Tapping for Public Speaking

Another area of great distress for students is public speaking. But fortunately there have been many clinical research trials on tapping for public speaking (I discuss many of them in *The Science Behind Tapping: A Proven Stress Management Technique for the Mind and Body*).

The main idea here is to think about how you feel at the thought of giving a talk. Write down all the emotions and thoughts that come to mind. If you or your child has an actual speech coming up, use that to think about. If you don't, just guess how you would feel if you did. The idea is to rate the amount of distress for each feeling out of 10 (10 = the most distress, 0 = none, very calm), and then tap through each of these one at a time. For example, if you were to feel extremely nervous, see if you can feel it somewhere in your body and then use that in your setup statement.

"Even though I feel so nervous about that talk, and feel sick in my stomach, I am open to being calm." The reminder phrase could be "so nervous, sick feeling."

Another idea is to think whether you (or your child) has ever had a negative experience with a past oral presentation or speech. If something went badly in the past, the nervousness can come from worrying it will happen again. The movie technique can be used to work through the past event. In this next story tapping practitioner Christine Wheeler helped an adult man who needed to give a speech at a wedding. No one knew how bad his fear of public speaking was, but he had even turned down jobs because of it. This story shows how a childhood experience can still affect you later in life.

* * *

Martin's fear of public speaking had been his quiet secret for years and a source of embarrassment at business meetings as he often found himself freezing when he was asked for his opinion about the matters at hand. He became very effective at evading meetings when he expected to be called upon, delegating the opportunity to one of his staff.

He had already turned down a promotion because the position involved presenting reports to his board of directors. Martin became a master at avoiding these opportunities to speak, and his colleagues did not know that he had a profound fear of public speaking. His closest friends didn't know of his fear of public speaking either.

One day Martin was blindsided by a request from his best friend to be the best man at his upcoming wedding. He knew that part of the responsibility of this honored position was to give a toast, and since he'd been best friends with the groom since childhood, he knew that everyone had great expectations of him. The wedding was months away, but Martin's fear, dread, and anticipation were overwhelming, so much so that he toyed with the idea of avoiding this opportunity as well. But he wrote a beautiful speech and practiced until he knew every word.

As soon as he practiced in front of his wife in their living room, however, he broke out into a cold sweat, his heart raced, and he kept forgetting his words. An audience of one was even too much for him, and having note cards didn't help as he lost his place constantly. And this was in his living room, in front of his wife. His anticipation of the actual wedding was off the charts, and he considered that he would rather lose his lifelong friend than expose himself to an audience of people watching him intently.

Fortunately, he confided in a friend who was a client of mine, and

Martin made several appointments with me by email. He was able to write about his "problem" in an email that he wanted me to read before the appointment because he was afraid that he couldn't even talk about it in my office. He was already feeling humiliated that this friend knew about his secret fear, and now he was sharing it with me as well. He was so agitated (his word) I assured him that we would do this as gently as possible, and we started the session by tapping on his current state, using words that he'd used to describe his current feelings and sensations. We tapped:

- *"Even though I am agitated right now because people know about my fear, I deeply and completely accept myself."*
- *"Even though I feel agitated in my stomach and am afraid of throwing up, I deeply and completely accept myself."*
- *"Even though I don't want to talk about my fear, I already emailed about it so maybe I don't have to and I deeply and completely accept myself anyway."*

His SUD level of intensity for this agitation had been at 10 on a scale of 0 to 10, and after these rounds it was at 3 out of 10. He was shocked that he felt that much calmer, and I pointed out that he was already learning how to calm himself with tapping. He said that he was really angry at himself and frustrated that he had this weakness. He was a successful person and avoided anything that might put him in front of an audience of more than one or two people. He hated being the center of attention that way. Since this is what came up, we tapped:

- *"Even though I am angry at myself for being so weak, I deeply and completely accept myself."*
- *"Even though I am frustrated that I have this weakness, it is humiliating, but I deeply and completely accept myself."*
- *"Even though I avoid anything where I am the center of attention, I deeply and completely accept myself."*

After a few rounds, Martin's sense of frustration and being angry at himself had eased, but he still had a 10 out of 10 charge on being the center of attention. I asked him about the last time he felt uncomfortable being the center of attention. He quickly had an event come to mind that had happened a few months previously, and just having it come to mind made him agitated again. Just thinking about telling me about it brought his agitation to 10 out of 10.

We started tapping before he started to tell me.

- *"Even though I am agitated just thinking about this story, I deeply and completely accept myself."*
- *"Even though I am afraid to freeze again if I think about this story too much, I deeply and completely accept myself."*
- *"Even though I feel weak because I have this story, I deeply and completely accept myself."*

He calmed to a level of intensity of 3 out of 10 and commented that he was starting to get that tapping might be working. He hadn't told anybody this story and reported that he felt he could talk about it with minimal discomfort. I asked him to start telling the story and to stop as soon as he noticed any discomfort and we would tap. He was at a party with friends (none of whom knew about his fear) and was talking to one friend about their fishing trip of the previous week. They were laughing about the big fish that got away from Martin, and their laughter got the attention of two friends standing close by. I saw Martin flinch a little and I stopped him and he said that the moment he realized that somebody else was listening to their laughter he started freaking out.
    We tapped:

- *"Even though I freaked out when Bob and Jerry turned to look at us laughing, I deeply and completely accept myself."*
- *"Even though I freaked out when we got their attention, I deeply and completely accept myself."*
- *"Even though I froze when they turned toward us, I deeply and completely accept myself."*

Martin's intensity moved from 7 out of 10 down to a 2, and he felt comfortable about continuing the story. But as soon as he considered what happened next, his level of intensity shot up again to 10 out of 10. At this point in the story, as the two friends were turning towards Martin, his fishing buddy said, "Hey Martin, tell them the story about the one that got away." Martin gasped and froze on the spot. We stopped and tapped:

- *"Even though my fishing buddy called them over and wrecked my fun, I deeply and completely accept myself."*
- *"Even though I froze when he called those guys over, I deeply and completely accept myself."*

- *"Even though I gasped and froze when he did that, I deeply and completely accept myself."*

Martin said that the intensity was calmer, but he had a memory of being a kid and his parents, who were very proud of him, encouraged him to practice playing piano while the two of them sat and listened and applauded. I find this happens quite regularly with clients when we start our session by tapping on the effect of a recent event; they spontaneously jump to a past event that they hadn't thought of in years. I asked Martin if something unpleasant had happened while he was playing piano.

He was surprised that emotions rose, and he began to tear up. We immediately tapped without a setup phrase on this surprising piano emotion. When Martin felt calmer, he recounted a typical piano practice after dinner, except this time his grandparents were visiting and were in the kitchen tidying up after dinner. They didn't know about Martin's after-dinner practices with his parents as an appreciative audience.

Martin was becoming more agitated as he told the story, but he said he wanted to get it out, and so we tapped after he finished the story. He said that he had been sitting happily playing for his parents when his grandfather stormed into the room yelling, "What is that awful noise?" Martin remembers in that moment freezing, stunned at his grandfather's attack.

At this point, Martin was crying in my office, so we tapped on the EFT points to calm him. Then we jumped into tapping on the parts of the event that he told me about. We tapped:

- *"Even though my grouchy grandfather yelled while I was playing and I froze, I deeply and completely accept myself."*
- *"Even though my grandfather said my playing was an awful noise, I deeply and completely accept myself."*
- *"Even though I was so scared when he yelled, it wasn't good to make him yell, I deeply and completely accept myself."*
- *"Even though my grandfather was a grouch and hated piano, it felt like he hated me, I deeply and completely accept myself."*
- *"Even though it wasn't safe to be the center of attention in case someone else can hear you, I deeply and completely accept myself."*
- *"Even though I froze when he yelled, I can thaw out now, I deeply and completely accept myself."*

Martin had no idea that his current fear of public speaking could be linked to that episode. For the first time in that session, I asked about his upcoming role as best man. Martin took a moment, and his eyes were shifting back and forth as if he was looking for the "problem." He said that this was the first time he didn't get a wave of sweating and a lump in his throat just thinking about it. He said he felt butterflies and some moths in his stomach at a level of intensity of about 6 out of 10. He was shocked at the improvement and reminded me that he'd emailed me the details of the problem. We tapped on his role of best man and giving the speech in particular. We tapped:

- *"Even though I am afraid to be the center attention in two months at Kevin's wedding, I deeply and completely accept myself."*
- *"Even though I almost said no to being best man...."*
- *"Even though I have been so embarrassed by my fear, I am feeling surprisingly different now."*
- *"Even though I am afraid that my grandfather will yell at me while I'm giving my speech..." (Martin laughed at this.)*
- *"Even though I am afraid to give a speech, this is my best friend, I deeply and completely accept myself."*
- *"Even though my stomach clenches at the thought of giving the speech, I deeply and completely accept myself."*
- *"Even though there are butterflies and moths in my stomach when I think of the speech, I deeply and completely accept myself."*
- *"Even though I am afraid of being caught off guard when I give my speech, I deeply and completely accept myself."*
- *"Even though I don't know what to expect when I give my speech, maybe I'll actually like doing it."*
- *"Even though I loved playing piano for my parents until my grandfather yelled, maybe I am a natural performer."*

At the end of this session, Martin reported being able to think about the fishing story episode without any upset at all and in fact related the whole story to me and we both laughed. He also reported feeling very calm about his grandfather storming into the room and yelling. He was very surprised that the thought of being best man and giving a speech didn't have the same charge. It had gone from a level of intensity of 15 on a scale of 0 to 10 to about 4 out of 10, and he commented that the butterflies in his stomach might actually be excitement. I left him with homework to practice his best man speech in front of his wife and see how he felt and that we would do another appointment before the wedding if he felt he needed to.

I got this email a week later:

"Thank you so much for that EFT session. I feel like a different person. On the way home in the car by myself, I recited the whole wedding speech without missing a beat and even thought of other things to add to the speech. Later that night I asked my wife if I could practice in front of her again, but I hadn't told her that I'd done that session with you. She started to cry because she could see how I was actually enjoying myself. I know she was an audience of one, but that was a huge shift for me. Last week at work, I even attended a meeting that I had been planning to avoid, and I felt very calm. When my boss asked me a question, I just answered as if we were alone in the room!"

We agreed that he would come for an appointment before the wedding if he needed to. I knew the wedding date but didn't hear from Martin until that day had passed.

He sent another email:

"The weeks leading up to the wedding were so much fun and I really enjoyed being with my friend as his best man and not being distracted by the dreaded speech. I even taught him some tapping to help him with his own speech nervousness. At the wedding itself, not only did I give a great heartfelt speech, I did so without any notes. The whole room was in tears, and I even got a standing ovation. Well maybe the groom got the standing ovation, but I was so happy to think it was for me! On another note, I have applied for a new position in the company that I avoided for years because of the public speaking requirement. I simply am not afraid anymore, and if I do feel anxious, I know I can just tap. Thank you for your help."

* * *

What a wonderful outcome—but this is also a common outcome. As highlighted in Martin's story, tapping also works for performances such as musical recitals, or singing, or even athletic games. It is the same process: think about the performance in the future and tap on how you think you will feel or even perform. My own daughter had a piano exam some years ago and was becoming seriously stressed the closer it came. She had sat for these exams before, so we weren't sure what the issue was. She actually said the examiner was very lovely in the past and she had achieved excellent grades. So, I asked her to tap with me about her worry and nerves. She mostly felt it in her stomach as butterflies and a sick feeling. We tapped for about 10 minutes and then she felt calmer so we stopped.

The exam was a few weeks later. She came home that afternoon, and I asked how it went. She said she felt the butterflies straight away as soon as she entered the room and saw the examiner (the same lady as previous years), but they subsided very quickly. She completed her piano pieces and left. We received her results several weeks later, and she achieved 93 percent. I reminded her we had done some tapping on her nerves, but she just laughed and ran off.

Finally, on the topic of public speaking, I was asked in 2019 to give a TEDx talk on tapping. I wasn't that worried about the talk as I had been lecturing for years and knew we could use slides as prompts and typically there is a rolling text screen in front of you on stage. Imagine my horror when I learned that the venue did not have a tele-prompter, that we needed to know our speeches by heart, and that while the slides would be projected above our heads, we couldn't turn around to look at them due to the cameras recording.

I was a little concerned! So, I started to rehearse my talk a lot and tapped while I spoke it out loud. As I was learning the talk from my notes (I often tape speeches like this on the glass outside the shower but facing in, so I can practice while in there—my husband must learn my speeches too), I would tap as I was reading and speaking. It helped keep everything calm and for the speech to be more easily integrated into my memory!

On the rehearsal day I was feeling ok: I remembered the speech and clicked the slides at the right time. Tapping had helped! The next day was the actual event: hundreds of people in the audience, eight cameras, and only one take! I was backstage with the seven other speakers that day, and some of them started to shake. Others were crying. Their nerves were out of control. The topic was creating change, so all of us had different topics—i.e., no one knew anything about my topic of tapping! I stood at the head of the table and asked everyone to just copy me and I started to say:

"Even though I am freaking out about the TED talk I am about to give, I accept this is how I feel."

"Even though I feel sick because I have to give that speech in a few minutes, I accept this is how I feel."

"Even though I don't want to walk out there, I accept this is how I feel."

We tapped round after round until we were told the event was starting. Everyone was visibly calmer, although they had no idea really what I was doing. One of the organizers actually filmed it! We all got through the day, and the congratulatory high fives were abundant that night. Have any of them kept tapping? I have no idea, but it definitely helped on the day. It was a visible difference.

You can watch my TEDx talk on the official TED website; search "Is Therapy Facing a Revolution?"

* * *

Tapping and Sports Performance

An area that appeals to older students is using tapping for sporting and/or athletic activities and goals. It is often a very good way to build a bridge to something they want to achieve without them rolling their eyes at your weird tapping technique! I also like to show video footage to teens of famous athletes using tapping. On my YouTube channel (Dr. Peta Stapleton) you will find an Olympian, a baseball player, a rugby league player, and a race car driver—all tapping. These videos are great to show teens who may be skeptical and need some convincing to at least try tapping.

A local school reached out and asked if I would teach their senior students tapping for exam stress and the like. These students were heading into their final year of studies. I knew that one way to engage teens and have them at least be open to tapping was to talk to them about goal setting. Tapping can look unusual, and we were trying to not have them reject us too quickly! So we asked: Is there a goal you would like to achieve for school (or otherwise)? All of them had a goal.

With goal setting and tapping, we typically ask someone to write down their level of doubt the goal could come true (out of 10) and any reasons they think might be obstacles to achieving it. The students did this for each of their goals. Then we tap on the reasons they believe the goal won't come true and the level of doubt (to lower it).

One student wrote he wanted to return to playing competitive football. We asked: What would get in the way of this coming true? He listed:

- A previous shoulder injury that required surgery (he was worried he would re-injure the shoulder)
- Other teams knowing about his surgery (he was worried they would target his shoulder as a weakness and that he would be re-injured again)

His doubt he could return to play and not be injured or targeted by other teams was 10 out of 10. We tapped with him on the doubt first, then on the worry.

About six months later, and into the new year (which was those students' final senior year) I happened to be at the school again for another purpose. I asked the school principal whether that particular student was playing football again and he said yes. He was also surprised I asked as there didn't seem to be any reason he wouldn't be playing! I inquired if the student had been injured at all, and again the principal was surprised and said, "No not at all. He is a wonderful player and will go on to have a fantastic sports career if he wants!"

I had a quiet laugh to myself and was so happy to hear this outcome.

• • •

This story by tapping practitioner Laura Campbell reveals how tapping can be used to improve sports performance in younger students too. It might just be that EFT is a secret weapon for athletes.

* * *

My 12-year-old daughter plays soccer on a fairly new team. They played in a tournament this weekend. My daughter hurt her leg in the first game Saturday, so I was trying to get her to tap on it. She was embarrassed in front of her friends, but one of them asked me to show her how to do it. All the girls were sitting on the ground in front of me and, as I demonstrated for one, they all began to tap.

Their next game was against a team that usually beats them by eight or nine points (in soccer, that's a slaughter). Some of them were intimidated prior to tapping. At halftime, they were ahead 1–0. My daughter came in the second half and yelled at me: "Mom, we tapped and we're winning." She later told me they even tapped at halftime (she knows how to do it). All the parents were raving about how great the girls were playing. They lost the game 2–1, but they never gave up and played with "heart."

They tapped before their first game on Sunday and won. They had 15 minutes before they had to play an undefeated team in first place in the tournament. The coach even asked me to do that "meditation thing you did" before the last game. I led them in tapping for their tension and sore muscles and then for best performance. I did get them to do 9 gamut to help them focus. [The 9 Gamut Procedure was part of the original Tapping process and involves 9 actions performed while tapping the "gamut" point on the back of the hand. It includes behaviors designed to engage both the left and right hemispheres of the brain, as well as eye movements.] *They played another excellent game, never gave up, and lost by only two scores.*

Now, did EFT make a difference? I think so. They all played better than I've seen them play: fewer mistakes, better coordination, got their foot on the ball, ran hard, had fun! Granted, this is not scientific evidence, but it's interesting.

* * *

EFT and Learning Concerns

There has been a case study completed on how EFT can be used for dyslexia (a learning condition that is evident in reading, comprehension, spelling, and writing). Often the condition causes a child emotional distress as well. While this study is a single case study (often useful as the basis for larger trials), it is a starting point to learn what works and what doesn't and is worthy of note.

Fiona McCallion, a London therapist,[1] worked with a woman in her twenties who suffered from dyslexia and had sequencing, disorientation, and emotional feelings attached to it. They had three sessions and addressed all of these areas with EFT. They started with past memories of teachers who had ridiculed her in class when she was younger.

The second session focused on two specific incidents involving two teachers at school. One was a math class where she was not given the marks for correct answers, because she couldn't explain the method she used to arrive at them. While she received marks for an incorrect answer (based on the method used), when she got the answer right, she got zero marks because she couldn't explain the method. You can imagine how confusing this might be for a child.

By the end of the three EFT sessions, the client was able to read easily and fluently, and understand sentences. The disorientation associated with the client's dyslexia had also reduced significantly to a point where it was no longer an issue. Using tapping to explore and assist with emotional distress attached to learning concerns is therefore highly recommended, and the applications in these settings may be boundless.

Learning a Language with Tapping

I want to finish with an interesting topic. As mentioned, tapping for learning can be used at all ages. Often an area where limiting beliefs abound is learning a new language as an adult. Most people believe it is very hard to do this as an adult; it is easier if you are a child. But what if you have tapping? Dr. Dawson Church of EFT Universe (a training organization) shares his story of learning Spanish as an adult.

* * *

I've been "trying to learn Spanish" for many years, less than half-heartedly. I bought a cassette tape language course (remember cassette tapes, steam locomotives, and other ancient technologies?) many years back, but it just melted in the sun on the dashboard of my car, never used. I've also always thought of myself as "one of those people who can't learn other languages easily," in contrast to some people who are effortlessly multilingual. I tried taking a Japanese course when I was in graduate school, and dropped the class because I found it too hard. I also tried a German class as an undergrad, with equally humiliating failure.

A year ago, several years into applying EFT in every facet of my life, I decided to try learning Spanish so I could speak to people in Mexico where I occasionally vacation. I bought some Conversational Spanish CDs, and began playing them in the car. I spend only about an hour a week in the car, in the form of three trips a week to and from the gym 10 minutes away, so I made slow, fragmented, and painful progress on the language CDs. It seemed like a waste of time.

Then, one day, I thought, "I wonder if I would learn faster using EFT?" I tapped while repeating the phrases, and though I could feel no difference in my body after tapping, my Spanish came along rapidly. Three months later, I spent two weeks in Mexico and spoke only Spanish the whole time.

I then decided to challenge my belief that "I'm not a natural at learning languages." I was due to deliver the keynote speech at the first Netherlands EFT conference, so I decided to learn Dutch while learning Spanish at the same time. This is quite a hard trick to pull off, but with the help of EFT, I have fun challenging myself. It is quite difficult to not mix up "Por Favor" with "As't U Bleeft" when you're learning both together!

I found Dutch utterly baffling but tapped away my frustration as I learned the phrases. Then, one day, the frustration just melted during EFT, and I began to "get" the language and enjoyed mastering the challenges. To my amazement, I flew through the Dutch course in a month, and the advanced Dutch CDs in a few hours, all while driving and tapping. Learning the new language required zero net time, since I was driving anyway. In the time I'd hoped to struggle through the first Introductory Dutch course, I was onto the second Intermediate Dutch series, all in just one hour per week, on average. Just tapping occasionally, while speaking, seemed to help me "get" the sense of these two very different languages, one in the Romance family of languages, the other in the Germanic family. I didn't use any setup or reminder phrases; I simply tapped the hand, torso and face points while I said the required words.

Nowadays I can't wait to get in the car and turn on the language lessons. I've decided to learn at least one new language a year from now on, starting with Chinese. Since I have virtually no free time as I travel constantly researching and teaching EFT, my hour a week in the car is my only opportunity. But I am now convinced that something about EFT relaxes the body and makes the mind receptive. The frustration usually associated with learning new skills can then dissolve, and you can make quick progress.

I hypothesize that EFT helps learning in two ways: it works(1) psychologically by removing the uneasiness and emotional resistance that sometimes accompany novel experiences and (2) physically by facilitating the acquisition of new neural pathways in the brain, a process known as neurogenesis.

* * *

I don't know about you, but I am very keen to try this with a language! One of our daughters has a personal goal to be multilingual (I don't know where this goal came from), and this may be the key to it being easier.

I hope this chapter has given you some interesting ideas for how to use tapping to supercharge the learning process. Whether you have a child in school now or one yet to start, or you are an adult wanting to process some events that happened in your past, tapping can be a wonderful addition to the process. Keeping the body calm does wonders to the brain and applied to anything you are learning may just make it that much easier. I only wish I had tapping in my schooling years. I was a nervous speaker and, despite being the school captain in my senior years, I couldn't give a speech without physically shaking. I didn't know tapping then, so I just gritted my teeth and got through it. The shaking was obvious, though! As an adult and after learning tapping, I did use it for this and now speak worldwide on stages, without shaking! No teeth clenching either.

Quick Action Steps

1. Think back to when you were in school. Did you ever have an exam, a performance, or something similar where you "forgot" what you knew? Write down how you felt then and how you feel now thinking back, and give those emotions a rating out of 10. Spend 10 minutes tapping as you think about the memory (like on a movie screen) so you are watching yourself at that younger age in the movie. See if the emotion reduces.

2. Do you have a child in your life you can teach how to tap as they are learning something new? See if it makes learning fun!

The next chapter is all about getting older. If you have ever heard (or even believe yourself) that memory begins to deteriorate with age, then prepare to change this belief! Tapping can be used to assist memory during the older years, and even improve it.

CHAPTER 5

Tapping for Memory
Loss and Aging

A common complaint as someone ages is that their memory is not what it used to be. Older adults might even find that medical professionals share this belief too: memory declines as you age. But have you ever stopped to wonder if this is actually true? Could this belief be an old wives' tale, open to change? From previous chapters we do know that beliefs about memory have an enormous effect on what we *actually* recall. If you were to believe you had a fantastic memory, even in older age, would you actually have a fantastic memory?

Would you believe that beliefs about poor memory ability can actually *cause* poor memory?!

Now while changes in the structure and function of the brain over time can affect cognitive processes, and health or medical conditions such as diabetes or high blood pressure or depression can interfere as well, myths about aging can contribute to a failing memory. Harvard Health has indicated that middle-aged and older learners do worse on memory tasks when they're exposed to negative stereotypes about aging and memory, and better when the messages are positive about memory preservation into old age.[1] They suggest that if you believe you are not in control of your memory function, then you are less likely to work at maintaining or improving your memory skills.

Hypnotherapist Christine Wesson points this out to her clients. She says:

The trouble is that you, like everyone else, have probably been influenced by the Western belief that at a certain age people become forgetful. If you are honest with yourself, you'll remember that you forgot things at age 16, at age 21, at age 35 and at age 46. The difference between then and now is that when you were younger you didn't put it down to age. You may have put it down to being busy, having too much to think about, or many other innumerable reasons. Then you reached a certain point in your life when you started to put forget-fulness down to age. As you focused on not having the same mental capacity as before, that became your reality.

The good news is that this can actually be improved with tapping.

Christine offers a very thorough approach here with her clients, and she begins with a story.

* * *

Imagine a person of your age 70 years ago. More than likely they would have lived in the same area, if not the same street, all their lives. Odds are they worked for the same company, doing the same job for all of their working life or, if female, were a housewife. The amount of new people they came into contact with was, in all probability, mini-mal. Most of those they met daily had been known to them for many years. There was no TV, no video, no telephones, and no computers. In all likelihood they didn't have a car. They had probably never been abroad or come into contact with any language other than their own. They shopped for food at the corner shop where they knew the propri-etor and all the other customers. It was possible to tell the day of the week by the food that was on the table.

Now bring yourself forward to this moment in time and think about what you have to learn and cope with in your modern world. You are constantly bombarded with new information on a daily basis. You have to drive, find your way to new places. You have to learn all the new technology including mobile phones, computers, TV, and video. You are constantly meeting new people. Then there's the constantly changing legislation, even if it's just about the latest rules on wheelie bins and what you can and can't put in them. When you go shopping you are presented with an array of food choices that would overwhelm the housewife of the 1950s, yet you cope marvelously. The world around you is constantly changing, it's moving faster and faster all the time, and you are keeping up, aren't you? Yes, I know there are things you can't do yet, but that's because you either aren't interested or haven't applied yourself. Your memory, far from being bad, is actually fantas-tic. It has an unlimited capacity for learning and retention, and all you have to do is allow it to do "its" job. Yes, it's true, your memory is unlimited, and it will grow and retain information according to what-ever you tell it. Start telling yourself now that your memory is getting better and better every day. Tell yourself daily that you have an unlimited capacity for remembering things.

* * *

Let's spend some time now unpacking what it is people may believe about their memory and aging. (You could look back at what you wrote in Chapter 1 too.) What did you hear your own parents tell you as they were aging? What have you heard yourself say if you forget something? Do any of these sound familiar?

- "My short-term memory is terrible."
- "My memory is getting worse."
- "I have a memory like a sieve."
- "It's just old age."
- "I'm so old."

How many more can you add to this list? Now rate these out of 10. Ten stands for how much that statement feels really true for you, and 0 represents that it isn't true for you at all. Now let's get tapping. Choose a statement to start with (one that really feels true for you, at least 8 out of 10). Let's say the setup as you tap on the side of the hand point (substitute your actual statement in the statements below):

- "Even though I believe my short-term memory is so bad, I accept myself and this belief."
- "Even though I believe my memory is like a sieve, I accept myself and this belief."
- "Even though I believe my memory is getting worse with age, I accept myself and this belief."

Now tap through these acupoints while repeating:
Eyebrow: "I have a memory like a sieve."
Side of Eye: "My memory is getting worse."
Under Eye: "It's just old age."
Under Nose: "this belief"
Chin: "this memory problem"
Collarbone: "so frustrating"
Under Arm: "I can't remember anything anymore."
Top of Head: "such a bad memory"
Remember that if one of these phrases seems to fit better, just say that one over and over (you don't need to change them on every

74

acupoint). Check in with that belief you rated at the beginning: how does it feel now out of 10? Keep tapping until you feel a reduction or the belief doesn't seem to have such a hold on you anymore. You might begin thinking "maybe I could have a good memory!"

The next step is to be open to the possibly you could have a good or even great memory, as you become older! Try this with the choices ending:

- "Even though I've been talking myself into having a bad memory, I choose to realize that I have a great memory."
- "Even though I have been hard wiring the idea that my memory is getting worse, I choose now to change this!"
- "Even though I have been focusing on having a bad memory as I get older, I choose to be open to having a fantastic memory instead!"

Let's tap through the eight points:

Eyebrow: "I choose to have a great memory."

Side of Eye: "My memory is getting better and better each day."

Under Eye: "I can easily change."

Under Nose: "What if I had a great memory?"

Chin: "I am open to having a fantastic memory."

Collarbone: "I can feel the possibilities!"

Under Arm: "I can easily remember."

Top of Head: "Such a fantastic memory!"

See how you feel after some rounds of tapping using the choices approach. If any doubt or disbelief creeps in and you don't believe these ideas at all, it usually means you have moved too quickly to the new belief. You can rate your doubt as per Chapter 3 and tap on the tailenders there about believing that you have a fantastic memory, and also go back and tap on what you do believe: that your memory is getting worse. Spend longer reducing the charge on what you do believe, until it no longer has a strong hold. Then start tapping with the new beliefs.

The Impact of Stress and Aging

Have you ever heard the term "the sandwich generation"? It is a term to describe those adults in a stage of life where they have responsibilities to children who still depend on them and also to their aging parents who may also require their help. They are literally sandwiched in between two other generations. Adults in this group are particularly vulnerable to extra stress in their lives since they have multiple roles. This is a stage where they might begin to show signs of memory loss (e.g., everyday issues such as names and words) but not acknowledge just how much this could be impacting their memory. It may be too easy to overlook these minor cognitive issues as being caused by stress.

When adults in their senior years lose a spouse or partner and start having to look after themselves, perhaps handle the finances, run a household, and even drive by themselves without support, they may show signs of cognitive decline. Families may make an assumption that they are showing signs of dementia (and a specialized assessment is always recommended to verify this), but it may also be a symptom of stress. It may be worth helping older adults with the stress in their lives prior to making assumptions.

In Chapter 9 there is a tapping plan for life, and you can use this to target beliefs about aging and failing memory in there too. Interestingly there has been research conducted on aging and how beliefs impact our bodies in general. Dr. Ellen Langer pioneered this in the 1980s. This is food for thought as you ponder beliefs about memory and aging!

The Counterclockwise Study

In 1981 Professor Ellen Langer from Harvard University led a study to investigate how aging is impacted by beliefs. She recruited eight men in their seventies and eighties and had them attend a five-day retreat at a monastery in New Hampshire. Members of the first group stayed for one week and were asked to pretend they were young men, once again living in the 1950s (22 years earlier). The second group arrived the week afterward, and members were told to stay in the present and simply reminisce about that time in their lives.

The monastery was set up as though it were the early 1950s: issues of *Life* magazine and the *Saturday Evening Post* were available to read, there was a black-and-white television on which to watch 1950s shows, and vintage radios played music from the era.

Both groups were assessed—they had cognitive and physical tests carried out—before and after their week at the monastery. Both groups became stronger and more flexible—after only one week. Height, weight, gait, posture, hearing, vision, and performance on intelligence tests also improved. The men's joints were more flexible, their shoulders wider, their fingers not only more agile, but longer and less gnarled by arthritis. Some of the men were even playing touch football by the end of the five days!

But the men who had acted as if they were actually back in 1959 and not just reminiscing showed significantly more improvement. Those who had impersonated their younger selves seemed to have bodies that actually were younger. Langer has been quoted, "Wherever you put the mind, the body will follow." The physiological results provided evidence for a simple fact: the aging process is indeed less fixed than most people think. You can read about the study and the outcomes in the book *Counterclockwise: Mindful Health and the Power of Possibility.*[2]

Imagine that tapping could support this process for yourself. What if the whole aging process, including the impact on memory, was able to be changed too?

Just for fun, and because memory issues don't only affect us when we age—children can use tapping for this too—Rosa Graham shares how her granddaughter couldn't recall where she left her phone.

* * *

My 11-year-old granddaughter Olivia and I enjoy reading about tapping; I like the articles about aches and pains and phobias; she likes the ones about children and pets.

So, when her cell phone had been missing for days, she suggested we try tapping. I love that she's always so willing to explore and test things out for herself, so I agreed immediately. Besides, I, too, was curious to see what would happen.

First, she tapped herself saying, "Even though I've lost my cell phone again, I'm still an OK kid." After a round or two of that, she shrugged her shoulders as if to say nothing happened.

She wasn't ready to quit, though. "Why don't I try as if I am my cell phone?" she asked. Again, I agreed. She tapped again, this time saying, "I'm lost, and I don't know where I am." A few more rounds of that and still nothing. I asked her if any images or thoughts came to her while she was tapping, and she shook her head no.

"Let me try," I suggested. After a few times saying, "I am Olivia's cell phone," I started tapping. I barely got the first sentence out of my mouth—"I'm lost, and I can't find Olivia"— when she bolted out of the room like a shot. A few seconds later she returned, beaming a big smile and holding up her lost cell phone!

She had suddenly remembered where she had put it. She had carried it into her mom's bedroom, and it had fallen off the nightstand and under the bed. We both laughed with amazement! And this grandma beamed with pride at how a little girl used tapping to solve her problem of a lost cell phone.

* * *

Using and Learning New Technology

Technology has changed our lives in recent decades, and it seems that every day there are new software, apps, programs, and updates to install! Passwords need to be regularly updated and levels of authentication seem to become more complex every month. Does anyone relate to this? I have heard my own parents and other older members of the community complain about trying to learn and stay up to date with these changes, and I agree that it can be overwhelming!

Sometimes our beliefs can interfere with our ability to learn new things, however, and feelings such as frustration and stress can then impact how easy a new skill could be. It might seem easier to ask a young teen in your life to update your software or change the password, but what if tapping could also help? Digital services and platforms might actually be helpful for connection and support—if only they were easy to use!

If you were to write down any beliefs or feelings about learning and using technology, what would you write? Do any of these feel true for you?

- There is not enough instruction and guidance to use technology (the manual is so hard to read!).
- I don't know enough about it to use it.

- I don't feel confident.
- I am too old to learn these new technologies.
- It's all too complex.
- I worry about whether the technology is safe.
- I don't like internet banking.
- I wish things would be the same as the old days.
- I can't remember my passwords.

Here are two examples you can tap for. It is just about being calmer around technology and staying open to the possibility that you might be able to successfully engage with and use it for your own benefit.

Topic: *I don't feel confident using technology. It's too hard.* (As you read this, rate your own confidence out of 10.)

Setup statements: Say these while tapping on the side of the hand point.

- "Even though I don't feel confident using technology, I accept that this is how I feel."
- "Even though I don't feel confident with all the updates and software changes, I am open to feeling better."
- "Even though I don't feel confident and believe it's all too hard, I am staying open."

Reminder phrases:
Eyebrow: "It's too hard."
Side of Eye: "don't feel confident"
Under Eye: "not confident"
Under Nose: "too hard"
Chin: "feel silly"
Collarbone: "feel dumb"
Under Arm: "not confident"
Top of Head: "too hard"

Keep tapping through the points until you feel a shift in the feeling or your thoughts. If anything new comes to mind (e.g., another feeling), then tap on that too.

Then try some tapping with these phrases:
Eyebrow: "Maybe I can be open."
Side of Eye: "What if it isn't that hard?"
Under Eye: "What if I could feel confident?"
Under Nose: "Maybe I could learn."

Chin: "Maybe I could do this."
Collarbone: "What if I could stay open?"
Under Arm: "Maybe it doesn't have to be hard."
Top of Head: "I am open to learning."

See how that feels when you tap on the possibilities. Make a note of anything that comes up. If you start tapping on the positives and your mind rejects this and you think "There's no way! That's not possible!" then it is better to keep tapping on the worry, frustration, and negative beliefs before moving on to more positive statements. Introducing the positive like this (and choice) is a good way to see if you are ready to think differently and have a new experience.

Let's try another one for remembering passwords!

Topic: *I can't remember my passwords! It's too hard.* (As you read this, rate your own feelings out of 10.)

Setup statements: Say these while tapping on the side of the hand point.

- "Even though I can't easily remember my passwords, I accept that this is how I feel."
- "Even though I feel frustrated trying to remember ALL my passwords, I am open to feeling better."
- "Even though it is so hard to remember all the different passwords, I am staying open."

Reminder phrases:
Eyebrow: "It's too hard."
Side of Eye: "feel frustrated"
Under Eye: "not confident"
Under Nose: "too hard"
Chin: "so hard to remember"
Collarbone: "feel dumb"
Under Arm: "My memory is bad."
Top of Head: "so many to remember"

Keep tapping through the points until you feel a shift in the feeling or your thoughts. If there is a main feeling (e.g., frustrated), then tap on that until it reduces. If it is more about a belief (e.g., having a bad memory), then you can tap on that belief too (see Chapter 3).

Then try some tapping with these phrases:
Eyebrow: "Maybe I can easily remember."
Side of Eye: "What if it isn't that hard?"

Under Eye: "What if I could remember the passwords?"
Under Nose: "Maybe I could learn these easily."
Chin: "Maybe I could do this."
Collarbone: "What if I could stay open?"
Under Arm: "Maybe it doesn't have to be hard."
Top of Head: "I am open to easily remembering all my passwords."

* * *

Before ending this chapter and moving into how tapping can be used to support those suffering memory disorders and conditions, I want to share a story from a colleague who used tapping for memory loss. Arishma Singh, a software salesperson and tapping practitioner, found her memory was impacted by medication and illness, but she still had success using tapping. It shows how memory loss affected by external factors can still be lessened with tapping.

* * *

In 2019, I started experiencing excruciating nerve pain for no apparent reason. I was unable to move, walk, or look after myself. Doctors classified it as neuropathy, and I went through many tests with neurologists. The medications that I was given created further issues, where I began to hallucinate and felt this sensation that I was "dying." Suffice to say, I was unable to work for four months. I used tapping for pain management and also took care of my body.

When I returned to work, I found that I was struggling to remember some of the details of my work, such as scripts, client details, and aspects of account management. I am a software salesperson in my day job. Initially I thought this was just temporary setback because I had been out of work for a period of time. But then, one day, I was sitting with a client and my manager when I realized mid-sentence that not only had I forgotten what I was there for but also my manager's name. I used this specific incident to tap that evening:

"Even though I feel embarrassed that I forgot [manager name] during my meeting with [x client name] today, I deeply and completely accept myself."

My reminder phrases were: "This embarrassment I feel in my head," "all this embarrassment," "how can I forget such simple things."

My SUDS reduced the embarrassment from 10 to 2. Other layers of emotions came up, and I tapped on the intensity of these. I tapped on sensations I felt inside my head—"this empty space," "this black box," "I feel afraid, right now right I am ok."

I tapped every day after work, on whatever element I had forgotten, and the associated feelings—it stemmed from humiliation, embarrassment, fear, shame, and sadness that I was "losing it."

One of the incidents that came up was me being in hospital in 2008 when I was put under a lot of opioids like morphine for a prolonged period and then additional opioids. I did not realize that it was the beginning of me losing some of the short-term memory. I had never worked on that before. Digging deeper into layers, I found out that I was unconsciously trying to "not remember" some of the memories from childhood that were too painful to be aware of. Once I uncovered the deeper issues, I worked with another practitioner to go through some trauma incidents with her.

I noted that, after three or four months, my short-term memory improved. I am luckily using an EFT practitioner currently to work through further layers.

* * *

So even when a medical condition or medications impact memory function (and many do), tapping may be able to assist with any strong feelings you have. If you ask yourself how you *feel* about your memory getting worse with age, then you can tap directly on that feeling. We know stress affects memory, but so do other emotions and behaviors. Stay open to the possibility that you can have a fantastic memory as you grow older!

Quick Action Steps

1. Think about a computer, software, or app-based program you have tried to use and found it difficult. What did you tell yourself about trying to use it? Do you easily remember your passwords to internet banking, logins for programs, and the like? Write down what you tell yourself about yourself and your beliefs and feelings. Technology is one area that rapidly shifts and grows and can overwhelm even the most tech-savvy person! Try some tapping to remember your passwords and about any programs that frustrate or overwhelm you.

2. In reading the last five chapters, have you had any other ideas come to mind about your own memory? Make a note so you can explore them further when you have time to tap. Even if you tap while thinking, it can be helpful.

This next chapter is a slight departure from the topic of memory issues, but it is nevertheless vital. It delves in three aspects of our lifestyles that affect memory and decision-making: sleep habits, sugar intake, and exercise. There is robust research to support tapping for these areas, and you will learn how to reduce sugar cravings, improve your sleep, and even potentially love exercise!

CHAPTER 6

Tapping for Sleep, Sugar, and Exercise

While so far this book has addressed common beliefs about memory, the aging process, and stress, the truth is that other external factors can affect your memory. Three that I want to discuss in this chapter can all be addressed with tapping: sleep habits, how much exercise you do, and how much sugar you eat. You may not have anticipated that this book would address these, but the reality is that more than a century of research has established the fact that sleep benefits the retention of memory.[1] Too much sugar consumption is linked to reduced memory and brain volume,[2] whereas physical exercise can improve cognitive abilities and enhance your mood.[3] If any of these three areas are not optimal in your life right now, then here's some guidance to apply tapping!

Tapping for Sleep Issues

As will be explored in Chapter 7, tapping has been investigated for sleep issues in elderly populations. But it is very useful to promote deep restful sleep in any age. You can use tapping if you have a hard time falling asleep (insomnia) or if you just can't seem to drift off. You may fall asleep easily but wake up in the middle of the night and not be able to go back to sleep for many hours. Tapping can help either of these situations. Here are your top tips to use tapping for sleep issues.

Always remember to be specific to your own physical sensation, using words to describe your situation or feelings/thoughts. Tapping works best when you are very specific.

Think about your own sleep habits. How does it make you feel if you don't sleep well or have issues sleeping at night? If you can feel it in your body, where is that? Make a note of where you might feel the effects of not sleeping well.

The second thing to think about is this: what do you tell yourself (your story) when you don't sleep? What thoughts are in your head (e.g., "I can't sleep," "I am a bad sleeper," "I will never sleep well")? Write these down as well.

Write the level of intensity on the ideas above out of 10, where 10 = the most intense feeling or sensation and 0 = completely calm. Tap through those ideas one at a time. Here is an example setup statement: "Even though I never sleep well and I always feel tired, I accept that this is the story I am telling myself."

Now for the reminder phrases. Tap through each of the points.

Eyebrow: "I feel so tired."

Side of Eye: "I never sleep well."

Under Eye: "I believe I am a poor sleeper."

Nose: "I feel so tired."

Chin: "This is the story I tell myself."

Collarbone: "I am SO tired."

Under Arm: "I never sleep well."

Top of Head: "What if this story could change?"

Tap through the points with the reminder phrase that seems to fit your situation the best and keep checking the SUDS out of 10. If the belief or story starts to feel less true, you know it is changing. It is then a matter of checking how you slept recently, and any other thoughts that come to mind.

There are two other ways you can use tapping for sleep issues. You can tap at night before going to sleep or if you wake in the night—just tap on the physical sensations (e.g., mind is racing, can't get comfortable, worry about sleeping well) to introduce some calm. You can simply tap and breathe (tap on each point but just say the words "breathe" or "relax" as you tap—this is to just introduce a physiological calm, rather than address any problem). You may then be in a position to start tapping on what is actually happening to interfere with your sleep.

As mentioned, it may be worth using tapping to explore why you don't have a great relationship with sleep. Have a think about when you may have started having sleep issues in order to track the pattern of when it started. If it is an adult behavior, try to pinpoint when it started and what was happening in your life (that will become the issue to tap on). If you had sleep issues as a child, think about how it was handled by your parents. I do highly recommend seeking the support of a professional and skilled tapping practitioner if you need support with this.

Here are some examples of what people may tap on:

- "Even though I feel stressed about my insomnia, I accept myself anyway."
- "Even though I never get enough sleep and feel [insert feeling] the next day, I accept how I feel."
- "Even though I feel overwhelmed, tired, and exhausted because I never get enough sleep ... I accept that this is how I feel right now."

The reminder phrases might include:

Eyebrow: "I feel so tired."

Side of Eye: "I'm feeling overwhelmed."

Under Eye: "I feel angry at my sleep issues."

Nose: "I feel stressed."

Chin: "This is overwhelming."

Collarbone: "I am SO exhausted."

Under Arm: "I feel worried."

Top of Head: "I don't know how to change all of this."

Tap and see how your body feels after a few rounds. Try to identify areas that might be holding tension, emotions, or anxiety. Keep tapping until you are a 0 or a 1 out of 10. Write down your notes to check in later. In Chapters 3 and 4 I discussed discreet tapping and using the fingernail points. These are great to use while lying in bed if you wake up and don't want to actively tap. Just squeeze or tap on the sides of the nail bed as you silently repeat the setup statements and reminder phrases.

* * *

This story is shared from Mary Anne Mohr, who used tapping to learn to sleep without over-the-counter sleep aids (which she had been taking for approximately 20 years).

The issue I chose to address was, "I've depended on sleep aids for over 20 years." When I asked myself how true this statement felt, the intensity level was a 10 out of 10. In other words, it was absolutely true. So, I began tapping on the side of the hand point, while speaking aloud: *"Even though I've depended on sleep aids for over 20 years and I know I was trying to control at least one aspect of my daily routine by having uninterrupted sleep, I truly and deeply love and accept myself. Even though I've depended on sleep aids for over 20 years and the pills helped me to close my mind off to anything I encountered that was stressful during that day, I truly and deeply love and accept myself. Even though I've depended on sleep aids for over 20 years and that is how I live my life today, I truly and deeply love and accept myself."*

I kept tapping while speaking reminder phrases: "This control of sleeping, taking sleeping aids, gives me uninterrupted sleep, I don't have to think before I fall asleep, I don't need to think of any stress I encountered during my day, I've been taking them for over 20 years, this control of sleeping, taking sleeping aids, gives me uninterrupted sleep, I don't have to think before I fall asleep, I don't need to think of any stress I encountered during my day, I have been taking sleep aids for over 20 years."

The thought "I have to take them, can't live without them" was an 8-out-of-10 intensity. To get more specific, I asked myself, "What does that issue feel like in my body?" It felt like pins and needles in my right foot (and was a 5 out of 10). I dug deeper: "What emotion is attached to that issue?" The answer was hopelessness and felt like a 9 out of 10.

Since this was the most intense aspect, I asked myself, "How do I know?" The answer came right away: "I feel right now I will never be able to sleep through the night without sleep aids." I then asked myself, "How true does that feel?" and it felt like a 9 out of 10.

The setup statements were: "Even though I know I will never be able to sleep through the night without sleep aids, I have pins and needles in my right foot and it is a 5 and I feel so hopeless and it is a 9, I truly and deeply love and accept myself. Even though this feeling in my body in my right foot, pins and needles, and it is a 5 and I feel the emotion of hopelessness, I truly and deeply love and accept myself. Even though, I feel hopelessness in taking sleep aids and it's a 9, I truly and deeply love and accept myself."

The reminder phrases were: "I can't sleep without sleep aids, I can't sleep without sleep aids, I feel so hopeless, I feel so hopeless, I have these pins and needles in my right foot. If I don't take my sleep aids I am afraid I'll be up all night worrying and thinking and I won't get any sleep."

I kept tapping: "I am afraid I'll be up all night; I am afraid I'll be up all night; I am afraid I will be up all night. I need my sleeping aids to sleep. I don't want to go to sleep without the sleep aids. I don't want to worry before I sleep. I don't want to think before I sleep. All this hopelessness in sleeping without aids."

The intensity level on "pins and needles in my right foot" went from 5 to a 1. The intensity level on "hopelessness" went from 9 to 7.

I asked myself, "What is going through my head now?" The answer I got was that I needed to try to reduce the two pills I take to one tonight, but I am scared I'll be miserable with no sleep, so I tapped on that!

To help myself get to the core issues, I asked myself if I could float back in time and remember a time I couldn't sleep for an extended period. The answer surprised me:

Wow. I just thought back to about 20 years ago and when I was offered a job in a new department. I went to the interview and the job was given to me. I didn't want a job handling public affairs issues for this company, and I didn't sleep for almost two weeks straight.

I felt hopelessness because I had no control of the situation and it was a 10 out of 10. I felt it in my lungs. I tapped on this until there was no more heaviness and it was a 0. I tapped on not wanting the job, not trusting my job share partner, and being forced to take the job with no choice (I was devastated). Eventually the shift occurred where this time in my life no longer had all these feelings attached.

Since all the tapping was specifically around my sleeping aids, I just tapped several rounds reducing my pills from two to one. The intensity went from 6 to 0. I successfully slept through using only one pill for five nights straight. The sixth night I slept through my first of many nights without any sleep aids.

Approximately seven weeks later, I have had no sleeping pills. I have slept soundly every night.

* * *

What a fantastic outcome for Mary, and a great illustration of asking yourself whether there has been another time in your life where sleeping soundly was an issue. Always remember you can seek the support of a professional to assist.

Let's turn now to physical exercise and how improving that might assist with your memory.

Tapping for Physical Exercise

The National Institute on Aging neuroscientist Dr. Henriette van Praag has said, "Overall, the message is that a consistently healthy lifestyle pays off." Their 2016 study showed that when muscles are exercised, they produce a protein called cathepsin B. It travels to the brain and triggers nerve cell growth in the hippocampus (critical for the creation of new memories, the hippocampus is also one of the first regions of the brain to deteriorate as we get older).[4]

Harvard University recommends establishing exercise as a habit, too, and to keep in mind that it takes about six months to start reaping the cognitive benefits of exercise. But after that, it is ideal to keep exercising for life.[5] With all the evidence and knowledge about how good exercise is in general, it begs the question why many people don't engage in any!

From 2011 (for 12 years) my research team and I conducted clinical trials using Tapping for food cravings, weight loss and emotional eating. From our food craving and weight-loss trial using tapping, we found that there were very common reasons people shared about not exercising. As you read this list, check off the ones that seem true for you (and then rate how strong they feel out of 10, where 10 = extremely true and 0 = not true at all).

- I hate exercise.
- Exercise makes you tired.
- I don't have enough time to exercise.
- It costs too much money to exercise and stay fit (e.g., going to a gym).
- I have no motivation to exercise.
- I feel stupid exercising.
- My body shape or weight prevents me from starting to exercise.
- I can't find an exercise I enjoy.

Targeting any of these beliefs with tapping to reduce their intensity may result in you finding an activity or exercise you enjoy doing, as well as the time to do it. If the objections have been removed, or no longer feel true for you, then you tend to be more open to enjoying exercise (and something may come along that you do enjoy). Here are some setup statements to show you what people tap on, and the reminder phrases. Tailor them to suit your beliefs and feelings.

Setup Statements:

- "Even though I loathe exercising, I accept myself."
- "Even though I feel fatigued and too tired to exercise, I choose to know that my energy levels will improve as I get fitter and I choose to be fit and healthy anyway."
- "Even though exercise feels like punishment, I choose to know that it will help me and I accept myself anyway."
- "Even though I have no motivation to exercise, I accept that this is how I feel."
- "Even though I'd rather eat than jog, I accept that this is how I feel but tapping may help."
- "Even though exercise frightens me because I expect to get hurt or sore, I choose to know that it will help me."
- "Even though I don't want to get too sweaty/hate getting sweaty, I completely accept myself."
- "Even though I'm afraid I'll look too muscly and big, I choose to know that it's in my imagination and tap anyway."
- "Even though I feel people think I look silly exercising, I choose to know that it's in my imagination and am tapping on this now."

Reminder phrases may include:

- "loathe exercise"
- "hate exercise"
- "feel too tired"
- "feel fatigued"
- "choose to be fitter"
- "choose to know I'll improve"
- "it's too hard."
- "feels like punishment"
- "no motivation"
- "no energy"
- "I feel too tired."
- "rather eat"
- "hate jogging"
- "don't want to"
- "Exercise frightens me."

- "It's scary."
- "It might hurt."
- "hate getting sweaty"
- "It feels yucky."
- "too sweaty"
- "Exercise makes you big."
- "too muscly"
- "I'll look silly."
- "Everyone will look at me."
- "I'll be embarrassed."

Tap through some of those setup statements and see how you feel after. You may not rush out the door to run several miles, but if you reduce any dislike of exercise, you will be more open to finding something that will work for you. Let's have a look at how tapping practitioner Carol Solomon helped a client with resistance to exercising. There were also other issues at play here.

* * *

My clients often develop resistance to exercise. They want to exercise, but either they don't feel motivated or don't enjoy it. They know they "should" exercise, but it can easily turn into an internal power struggle.

There can be other obstacles to overcome as well. Some women feel embarrassed, ashamed and/or self-conscious to go the gym at their current weight. So, they avoid the activity that could actually help them lose weight. Others have perfectionist qualities; they think it won't make a difference, or it's not "worth it" unless they have time for a full 60-minute workout. So, they don't go at all.

My client "Susan" wanted to talk about her resistance to going to the gym. She started out "I love it ... and I know I should do it, but it's not part of my routine.... I need to make a plan." My intuition told me that there was something deeper. I said, "Susan, it's not about planning." She said, "Why should I get excited or feel positive about anything? You know the other shoe is going to drop."

Two years ago, Susan's husband died while undergoing a routine sinus surgery. She had pulled her life together and even began a new relationship. One week before this session, her new beau had been diagnosed with colon cancer. It was no wonder that Susan felt as she did.

- *"Even though I don't want to get excited about anything because I know the other shoe is going to drop...."*
- *"Even though nothing turns out right for me, I choose to move forward anyway."*
- *"Even though everything always gets messed up...."*

Eyebrow: "Why should I get excited?"
Side of Eye: "I know the other shoe is going to drop."
Under the Eye: "Things never turn out right for me."
Under the Nose: "Why bother?"
Chin: "I feel cursed."
Collarbone: "It's not fair."
Under the Arm: "I've tried so hard."
Top of Head: "Everything always gets messed up."

Susan was also worried that she wouldn't keep up her momentum. In the two years since her husband's death, she had one crisis after another and couldn't follow through in her usual manner. Several attempts to make changes in her career got derailed when multiple crises occurred.

- *"Even though I'm afraid I'll lose my momentum again...."*
- *"Even though I'm afraid I won't be able to maintain it...."*
- *"Even though I'm afraid something will happen, I choose to move forward anyway."*

Eyebrow: "I've tried so hard."
Side of Eye: "Everything's a crisis."
Under the Eye: "I'm afraid something will happen."
Under the Nose: "I'll just lose momentum again."
Chin: "I won't be able to maintain it."
Collarbone: "I'm not going to do it."
Under the Arm: "You can't make me."
Top of Head: "I don't want to be disappointed again."
We tapped:
Eyebrow: "I choose to release these fears."
Side of Eye: "I choose to move forward."
Under the Eye: "I choose peace."
Under the Nose: "I choose happiness."
Chin: "I choose serenity."
Collarbone: "I am grateful for all of the opportunities in my life."

Under the Arm: "I choose to let it be fun and easy."
Top of Head: "I can handle whatever comes."
Since that session (two rounds of EFT), Susan began exercising
with ease every day. She has also started a website and moved for-
ward with significant changes in her career. These are the miracles we
see with EFT every day.

* * *

As Cathy points out, sometimes the reasons surrounding our blocks are not obvious. Tapping was used to support Susan in finding her reasons, processing them with an expert, and getting the outcome she wanted today (enjoying exercise!). The last section here is devoted to another lifestyle factor that can have a profound impact on memory: sugar intake. My decades of research into tapping for food cravings has shown that the foods hardest to resist are sweet ones!

Tapping for Sweet Foods

At an ancestral level, our primitive forebears learned quickly that sweet and sugary foods were excellent sources of energy. We now find sweet foods particularly pleasurable in our modern day, and when you eat them the brain's reward system activates. The issue is that high sugar consumption causes inflammation in the brain, leading to memory difficulties.[6] High rates of sugar intake are associated with depression,[7] and frequent exposure can shrink your brain size, leading to memory difficulties.

Most people admit their sugar intake could be a little high but also say how hard it is to avoid. Sugar intake has been likened to substance addictions because of the similar effects in the brain that cause cravings. So it can be a very real battle to avoid it!

The one research area I have investigated the most with tapping is how to apply it to food cravings, not only to lose weight but to lose the desire for trigger foods so you do not even think about them anymore! And this is exactly what happens in our trials. A year and even two years later, people tell us they cannot recall what foods they tapped on, and when we remind them, they laugh and say they don't eat those anymore. What I love about applying tapping to food cravings is that you don't have to use willpower in the future. Here are my top tips to get you started.

If you do feel like you might be "addicted" to sugar (i.e., you love anything sugary and sweet), start with this setup statement (rate how much you desire sweet foods out of 10 too; 10 = most desire, 0 = no desire at all).

- "Even though I am addicted to sugar [or insert own food craving here], I choose to accept myself anyway."
- "Even though I love everything sweet, I accept that I feel this way."
- "Even though I crave this food after meals, I choose to accept myself anyway."

Your reminder phrases may include:

- "addicted"
- "love sugar"
- "I crave…."
- "I love…."
- "love sugary sweet foods/drinks"

Tap as much as you need to until there is some relief (a decrease in the intensity). Then, if you are able, select one food/drink you would like to reduce the desire for and have it in front of you. Write down as many words as you can to describe any smell or scent that is appealing. Write the descriptive words (e.g., *sweet*, *delicious*, *chocolaty*) and then rate how intense they are out of 10 (10 = most intense smell, 0 = no attractive smell at all). Tap on these one at a time until the smell or scent appears to change. You might tap on sweet smell first, then move on to delicious smell next, and so on.

Then write as many words down to describe the taste of this food/drink (you will need to taste it). These words may be different from those you wrote for smell. Rate these out of 10 and tap for them one at a time.

If you have tapped on the above and there is still some desire to eat/drink the item, write down any words to describe how you feel in your mouth, body, head, anywhere in your body when you eat/drink it. If it feels warm and soft in your mouth and it feels calming, write that down, rate it, and tap on those different feelings.

By this stage you may have achieved a reduction in desire for the food/drink. If you have zero desire, feel free to finish here. If there is still some desire, you can tap on "this remaining desire to want to eat/drink." You can also ask yourself: "Do I really want this desire to leave?" Is there a part of you that may feel deprived or even resentful if you can't eat/drink this item? You can tap on those feelings too. The feeling of deprivation when you think of going without is a common one. It is often why diets fail! Here are some common setup statements you can use:

- "Even though I feel deeply deprived if I don't have this [food/drink] anymore, I deeply and completely accept myself anyway."
- "Even though I feel angry that I am giving up [food/drink], I accept that I feel this way."
- "Even though I am resisting letting this desire for [food/drink] go, I accept that I feel like this."

Your reminder phrases may include:

- "afraid to let go"
- "afraid to change"
- "this resistance"
- "feel deprived"
- "feel angry"
- "feel resentful"

Other common topics that arise with food also include loneliness (food becomes the friend), anxiety and stress (food becomes a way to soothe yourself), family patterns (food is used as a reward), and even feelings such as boredom. Below are some setup statement examples for each of these areas to explore.

Loneliness

- "Even though I feel this deep loneliness, I accept that this is how I feel."
- "Even though I feel lonely and completely empty inside, I accept myself."
- "Even though I use food as my reliable friend because I feel so lonely, I accept myself anyway."

- "Even though food keeps me company and stops me being aware that I am alone and afraid, I accept that this is how I feel."

Anxiety and Stress

- "Even though I can't stop feeling anxious/can't control my anxiety, I completely accept myself."
- "Even though I know I tend to eat to relieve my feelings of anxiety or stress, I accept myself and am open to changing this."

Family Patterns

- "Even though my mother let me eat more cookies/sweets/chocolate/junk food whenever I cried, I choose to accept myself."
- "Even though my grandmother always overfed me to keep me quiet when I visited her, I choose to completely accept myself anyway."
- "Even though my mother gave me ice cream to distract me from feeling sad and disappointed when my friends wouldn't let me play, I accept my feelings now."
- "Even though my dad started to buy me chips to make me feel better when I was disappointed about losing the football match, I completely accept myself."
- "Even though I was fed to make me feel better when I was sick with ... I accept that this is the best they knew."

Boredom

- "Even though I used food as entertainment and to stop myself feeling bored, I accept myself anyway."
- "Even though I used food as security, I choose to accept myself anyway."
- "Even though I over-ate to distract myself from ... I accept myself anyway."

- "Even though I overate to avoid ... I accept that this is all I knew to cope."

Before we finish this chapter, I want to share a story from my colleague Dr. Carol Look, who is a master EFT practitioner. "Brenda" attended an EFT for anxiety relief class Carol hosted at a convention. As part of the agenda, she asked for volunteers for an in-class demonstration for food cravings and underlying feelings. Brenda was one of four volunteers.

* * *

Brenda chose the bag of M&M's from my pile of props, and she rated her cravings for them as an 8 on the 0–10 SUD Level of Intensity number scale with 10 being the highest.

Our first round of tapping was: "Even though I have these cravings, and I really love the way my favorite food tastes, I deeply and completely accept myself." Each person's 0–10 SUD level number on craving decreased.

One woman said her craving had gone down significantly and she was now thinking of the good times she had with her father. Brenda echoed this thought and reported feeling profound grief. She had lost her father when she was eight years old, and her mother couldn't handle her grief and crying so she gave Brenda food to shut her up.

All four volunteers associated their eating of junk foods with losses they had experienced. We tapped:

- *"Even though I feel deep grief and want to eat to cover it up, I deeply and completely accept myself."*
- *"Even though I feel these deep losses and I want to stuff myself with food, I deeply and completely accept myself anyway."*
- *"Even though I feel abandoned because they left me, I deeply and completely accept my feelings."*

The volunteers continued to unravel layers of sadness around the losses they had experienced. Brenda said that her craving for the M&M's was going down dramatically, but her feelings of sadness were surfacing strongly. She told the class that she had lost two children, a fiancé, and her favorite pet. She also reported having strong physical feelings of grief in her chest, "a bowling ball in my chest."

We tapped:

- *"Even though I use the sweets to feel better because I love how they make me feel, I choose to feel safe and comfortable without them."*
- *"Even though I can't get satisfied, I love myself anyway."*
- *"Even though sweets are the only thing that make me feel better, I deeply and completely accept myself."*

Brenda told the class that the "bowling ball feeling" in her chest, a heartache, was decreasing in intensity and moving down towards her solar plexus. We tapped:

- *"Even though I have suffered so many losses, I choose to feel accepting of myself and of them."*
- *"Even though I just want to be acknowledged for all my losses and how hard it's been, I deeply and completely love and accept my feelings."*

Brenda said this one really "hit" her hard. She realized that all she had wanted was to be acknowledged for all the pain that she had been through. She told the class that everyone sees her as such a strong person and that they assume things come easily to her.

We tapped several more rounds on grief and being acknowledged. We also tapped for Brenda's belief that whenever she gets close to someone, "they drop dead."

- *"Even though I don't feel safe getting close to someone, I choose to love and accept myself."*
- *"Even though I've suffered enough and don't need to suffer anymore, I deeply and completely love and forgive myself."*

Brenda said this last round released the tremendous pain she had been carrying around for so long. She heard herself say, "You're right, I've suffered enough" and felt free to let go of her deep grief at this point.

Four months later, I talked to Brenda to see how she was doing. She had been doing her own tapping during the first week but then stopped. She had not eaten any sweets since the class, including while she was on a weeklong vacation in Florida. Ice cream used to be her favorite comfort food, and she hadn't had any in four weeks.

On her birthday she only ate one bite of birthday cake, and she didn't like it because it tasted too sweet!

While in the class demonstration, Brenda used the bag of M&M's

as a symbol for all sweets in her life and was so pleased that it had obviously worked for cake and ice cream as well.

Brenda said she has not stepped on a scale yet, but that several people told her she looked as if she lost weight. She was ready now to deal fully with her weight issue, and reported that the tapping came at exactly the right time in her life.

* * *

I opened this chapter with the idea that tapping could also help with three areas that may affect memory. Targeting and tailoring your tapping as you address sleep habits, exercise activity, and sugar intake may not only improve your memory, focus, and concentration, but also make all three areas easier in your life. Not fighting with willpower to avoid sweet food, forcing yourself to exercise when you loathe it, or stressing over whether you will sleep well are great areas for tapping—even if you are not worried about your memory!

Here is one more story where EFT trainer and advanced practitioner Naomi Janzen benefited herself after assisting a client.

* * *

A current client in her seventies asked me for help with her brain fog and associated memory issues. We've been working on her chronic insomnia, and she has been sleeping better than ever before in her life. While we haven't worked directly on her memory, she's noticed that as the brain fog ebbs there are signs it, too, is improving.

Yesterday, I got into my car to start a two-hour drive to Sydney [Australia] and when I went to claw my prescription sunglasses down from their usual perch on top of my head, they weren't there. A top-to-bottom search of my house didn't produce them. I phoned a couple of the shops I'd been in the day before. Nothing turned in. Where the heck were they? I had no choice but to tap. "Even though I don't know where my sunglasses are ... or where I last had them ... and I must have had them when I drove home yesterday but where the heck are they now?" When I flashed on a split-second impression of pulling my sweater off over my head, I went into my bedroom and found the sweater on a chair. Shook it. Nothing. I was out of time so I grabbed my backup glasses and left. This morning I found my sunglasses on the floor where I had shaken my sweater. They had fallen out. I just hadn't seen them. Time to start tapping on my eyesight!

* * *

The next chapter extends the idea of other daily activities that impact memory: alcohol use, smoking, and blood pressure. But before we head there, have a look at the quick action steps below.

Quick Action Steps

1. Complete this sentence: "I am a ... sleeper." What do you believe about yourself in this area? If it is negative, can you rate that belief out of 10 and do some tapping to loosen its strength, in order to have better sleep?

2. What food/drink will you target today with the tapping sequence, to reduce the desire? Remember, after tapping, you won't need any willpower to avoid it. You just won't feel like having it.

CHAPTER 7

Tapping for Alcohol, Smoking, and Blood Pressure

As the previous chapter outlined, many lifestyle choices and behaviors can affect the quality of our memory and even impact memory loss. Three more for which we can use tapping are alcohol use, smoking, and blood pressure.

Like I outlined for food issues (especially sweet foods) in Chapter 6, tapping can be used to reduce quantity and frequency of alcohol intake, so let's start there.

Tapping for Alcohol Use

While alcohol is one of the most commonly used drugs (about 85 percent of Americans report they have drunk alcohol in their lifetime[1]), it seems it only takes five drinks to impact whether you will remember that night out.[2] Alcohol affects short-term memory more than long-term and slows down the nerve communication in your memory center, the hippocampus. It also seems that older adults are more vulnerable to these effects; as you age, alcohol affects your brain, which has become more sensitive. While it may not be severe enough to cause dementia, alcohol does stay in your system longer as you age, and if you are also taking medications for health concerns, these can interact and worsen the effect of alcohol.

So, if you are concerned about how much alcohol you are drinking, or want to reduce the frequency or quantity, tapping may help. If you need the support of an experienced practitioner to address this, I highly recommend seeking one out.

How we address this issue is similar to the food craving one. The first step is to identify how you feel about how much you drink, or how often. Read these statements and tick off the ones that resonate.

- I have cravings I can't resist.
- I feel stressed (about …), so I have to drink to calm down.
- I want to reward myself after a hard day.
- It's just a habit now.
- I don't even think about it; I just drink.
- I can't stop once I start.
- I always intend to have only one.
- I love the taste of ….

You can then have a look at how you feel the next day:

- I feel guilty after drinking.
- I feel ashamed.
- I feel regret.
- I feel awful.
- I can't remember what happened the night before.
- I feel bad.
- I feel embarrassed.
- I feel mortified.
- I feel awkward around others.
- I feel uncomfortable.
- I feel remorseful.
- I feel humiliated.
- I feel sorry.

Take one statement from the above lists, rate it out of 10 (10 = strongest feeling, 0 = neutral) and tap to reduce it. Here is an example:

- "Even though I always only intend to have only one glass, and I feel ashamed the next day when I didn't, I accept that this is how I feel."
- "Even though I have a craving for … but feel awful the next day, I accept that this is how I feel."
- "Even though I just want to reward myself for a hard day/week, I accept that this is how I feel."

The reminder phrases on each point might be:

- Eyebrow: "this craving"
- Side of Eye: "feel ashamed"
- Under Eye: "feel awful"
- Nose: "need to reward myself"

- Chin: "can't resist"
- Collarbone: "feel stressed"
- Under Arm: "strong craving"
- Top of Head: "bad habit"

Tapping can be used for the craving or urge (the same as for food) whereby you have the drink in front of you and tap for the aspects. This is usually best done at the time of day you would usually have the drink, as the sensations and desire are typically stronger. The aspects might be: the smell, the temperature of the drink, the taste in your mouth, the feeling in your body, the ritual, and so on. It is best to rate each one separately out of 10, and tap on them individually before moving to the next one.

Here is an example for taste. Rate the taste out of 10 (10 = strongest taste, 0 = neutral).

- "Even though this drink tastes refreshing and crisp in my mouth, I accept that this is how I feel."
- "Even though this taste is bubbly and fresh, I accept that this is how I feel."
- "Even though this drink tastes smooth and full in my mouth, I accept that this is how I feel."

The reminder phrases on each point might be:

- Eyebrow: "this taste"
- Side of Eye: "crisp and cool"
- Under Eye: "bubbly"
- Nose: "smooth"
- Chin: "fresh"
- Collarbone: "refreshing"
- Under Arm: "amazing taste"
- Top of Head: "taste in my mouth"

You would continue tapping on the taste until it reduced, and then move to the next sensation of the drink. The aim is for the drink to lose its power to induce craving. Sometimes taste is the strongest driver; sometimes it is the smell or feeling in your body. Tap on each of them from your list *one at a time*. The end result is a reduction in the intensity and craving or urge level, and you will feel more in control (not the alcohol controlling you). You may find the desire decreases and in future you aren't drawn to that drink as often or to drink as much.

One area I am not addressing here is addiction per se. Levels of drug/alcohol use that may meet the definition of addiction are best dealt with by professionals. One indicator may be that you try the above process and it has little effect on your desire level. Another may be that as you are tapping on sensations attached to the drink, other memories come to mind from childhood that may be distressing. Alcohol can be used to soothe deeper emotions from younger memories; an experienced practitioner can help sort this out.

Practitioner Colin Larcombe shares here his own personal story of tapping for alcohol.

* * *

I have been successfully using EFT on my own personal issues ever since I had testicular cancer at the tender age of 35. I have been successful in applying emotional freedom techniques for all the after-effects and unwanted thoughts that are associated with cancer and eliminating any troublesome thoughts that would reoccur.

I have had a meditation practice and I have been a yoga practitioner. I felt it was time to give up alcohol because it was not integrating well into my new healthy lifestyle. I exercise daily, and trying to get into the lotus position with a hangover was not the easiest thing to do at 6:00 a.m.

I would not say that I am an alcoholic. I drink maybe a glass of wine or beer a day, with a bit more for social drinking at parties and get-togethers. I have never been sick drunk, yet I held this fear that I couldn't stop drinking. My first drink was at the age of 13, and I mixed white wine and red wine at a party. The person who gave me the alcohol was my father. He is an alcoholic and drinks a bottle of alcohol a day.

I had several attempts at eliminating alcohol from my life, without success, until I tried applying emotional freedom techniques.

First, I tried tapping:

"Even though I feel awful after drinking, I deeply and completely accept myself."

"Even though drinking reduces my capacity to be a good husband and father, I deeply and completely accept myself."

"Even though I feel that it's my dad's fault that I started drinking in the first place, I deeply and completely accept myself."

"Even though I adore the taste of a cool beer, I deeply and completely accept myself."

104

"Even though I adore the taste of a chilled glass of white wine, I deeply and completely accept myself."

None of these seemed to work. I then thought about the fact that I drank for social reasons and the desire to fit in. Maybe I needed to tap on that.

I tapped:

"Even though I think that I will feel like an outcast if I don't drink, I deeply and completely accept myself."

"Even though I think that I will have no friends if I don't drink, I deeply and completely accept myself."

After working these two tapping statements at every occasion where alcohol was being served, I would ask myself: "Am I able to refuse this drink?"

Even though I was tapping, I still found that I would still give in and have a glass of wine or a beer. Then I would be once again frustrated at my lack of being able to give up this habit and fully embrace a healthy lifestyle.

My breakthrough finally came one evening when I found myself thinking about getting a beer while walking from my office to the train home.

I started tapping:

"Even though tapping feels like it is absolutely useless for these desires, I deeply and completely accept myself."

Strangely enough, this gave me comfort to believe that maybe tapping wouldn't work on my need to stop drinking. I saw how I could always blame tapping for the failure if I wanted, and then accepted, a drink. Needless to say, this time I didn't stop for a beer before my train ride home.

My final epiphany came some days later, when I was doing something unrelated. I had this vision of what I had always wanted alcohol to achieve for me, for example being able to sit down with my wife, on the sofa, in front of the fire with a cold glass of white wine, just chilling out and relaxing together.

But it had NEVER EVER happened that way.

I started to tap:

"Even though I have never been able to achieve the dream state I desire with using alcohol, I deeply and completely accept myself."

And that was it! The desire evaporated. I kept pinching myself as I kept tapping:

"Even though I can't believe I will never drink alcohol again, I deeply and completely accept myself."

I spent so much time concentrating on the negatives and the side issues of alcohol I didn't realize that it was the image of what alcohol was supposed to bring into my life that was the key to my cravings all along.

I have not had a drink since, nor the desire. I take each day as it comes now, but without the fear or the anxiety that I can't live a completely healthy life.

* * *

This story highlights that sometimes it is what alcohol is giving you rather than the negative effects of it. What we do know is that reducing quantity and frequency through tapping helps you feel more in control and you won't have to use willpower. And your memory may thank you!

Quitting Smoking Easily

Another lifestyle area that is not necessarily linked to memory issues is cigarette smoking. But research now indicates that quitting smoking can restore your memory to the same level as nonsmokers.[3] It appears the substances in tobacco and nicotine (there are actually more than 4,000 chemicals) build up in the brain and damage learning and memory areas. Long-term smoking interferes with your ability to remember everyday tasks (e.g., taking medication or paying a bill) and functions such as ignoring distractions and focusing on single tasks.[4] Smoking also affects your sleep quality (the chemicals again), which also then damages your memory capacity and function.

There are now some tapping studies that have helped people quit smoking without the need for substitution (e.g., nicotine replacement) and assisted with withdrawal symptoms. I conducted one such study in 2013.[5] Here are some common ways to apply tapping when quitting cigarettes.

Cigarettes as Tranquilizers?

People wishing to quit smoking admit that they use cigarettes to avoid, numb, or suppress a variety of feelings that are uncomfortable.

Some people use cigarettes to relax and calm down, some use them to give them an energy boost, while still others use them to feel safe or protected. When using tapping for smoking cessation, you need to investigate and address any underlying emotions that cause the person to reach for cigarettes. Tapping can be aimed at feelings of loneliness, emptiness, rejection, anger, fear, and so on. Once these underlying emotions are detected and treated with tapping, a person's cravings to smoke and numb these feelings are reduced or eliminated.

Withdrawal Symptoms

One of the biggest worries clients share before we begin the smoking cessation treatment is their fear of painful or uncomfortable withdrawal symptoms. We interpret withdrawal symptoms as the body's way of expressing anxiety, physically or emotionally, about giving up the drugs and chemicals in cigarettes. The body literally craves the drugs and nicotine, and friends might share war stories from when they went "cold turkey" and how awful it was. Tapping can be used for each specific symptom as well as the fear of the future and what withdrawal may feel like.

Favorite Times of Day to Smoke

When people quit on their own, they might fail to honor the intensity of physical and mental associations they have with cigarettes. These associations are so powerful that they can lead a person to sabotage any success as early as the first few days of quitting. Classic associations that must be addressed and treated include:

1. smoking while on the telephone,
2. smoking while in the car,
3. smoking after a meal and/or socializing with others,
4. smoking during stressful times, and
5. smoking before going to bed.

All of these emotional links can be eliminated with tapping while stress in general is being neutralized.

The Essential Questions!

Find a pen and write your answers to these two questions:

- What is the downside of quitting smoking?
- What is the upside of remaining a smoker?

The answers to these two questions must be uncovered for smokers to successfully quit. Examples of answers to question #1:

- I won't know what to do with my hands.
- I need the cigarettes for my identity.
- If I quit, I won't know how to relax.
- If I quit, I will have to achieve more.
- If I quit, "they" will expect too much from me.
- If I quit, I'll probably gain weight.

Examples of answers to question #2:

- If I remain a smoker, I can hide from others.
- If I keep smoking, I will remain thin.
- If I stay a smoker, I can get away from people when I smoke.
- If I keep smoking, I can clear my mind on a regular basis.
- If I keep smoking, I will be like my father.
- If I keep smoking, I'll feel better.

Let's have a look at some common setup statements to get your started:

- "Even though I can't quit since no one in my family has ever successfully quit, I accept myself."
- "Even though no one in my family has ever quit for good and therefore I can't quit, I accept that this is how I feel."
- "Even though I think it's my destiny to be a smoker … I accept this is what I think."

The reminder phrases could be:

- "I can't quit."
- "No one in my family has quit."
- "It's my destiny."
- "I'm stuck with it."

Here is another angle:

- "Even though I'm afraid to let go of this problem, I deeply and completely accept myself."

- "Even though I don't believe in myself, I accept that this is how I feel right now."
- "Even though I don't believe I can reach my goal, I am open to trying."

Your reminder phrases could be:

- "don't believe in myself"
- "can't reach my goal"
- "afraid"
- "don't believe"

As when dealing with food or alcohol cravings, it can be helpful to do some exposure therapy. Write down what happens when you pull out a cigarette and sit there holding it. Is it the smell (unlit)? Is it a feeling in your body you sense? If you go to light the cigarette, do it slowly so you can sense any feelings that might be present. Do you feel a sense of calm? Is there some relaxation response that is associated with the cigarette and lighting it?

For one male (34 years old) in our clinical research trial, the feeling of something in his mouth was uncovered during this process. He said, "I've tried to quit before and always ended up having three packets of soothers a day instead. I didn't realize how intense the need was to have something in my mouth." This is what he ended up tapping on: the need to have a feeling of something in his mouth.

Your Tapping Plan

In the research paper we published on our trial we included a tapping plan to quit smoking, and I am sharing it here. We recommend that you set yourself 10 to 20 minutes per day to tap on one or more of these issues and work your way through the plan systematically. Some of the issues may not apply to you. That's ok; move on. If you are not sure if that issue is yours, tap on it anyway. Make sure you do read all of them, though, and see if they resonate for you.

Six Common Areas to Address

1. Address and treat the limiting beliefs that block success and sabotage you.

Example setup statements for this topic include:

- "Even though I don't deserve/I'm not worthy of becoming a nonsmoker, I accept myself anyway."
- "Even though I don't deserve to succeed, I completely accept myself anyway."
- "Even though I don't deserve to be happy/successful, I accept that this is how I feel."

2. Address and treat the emotional themes that you may have around smoking.

This might include identifying if there are feelings of deprivation or abandonment if you quit smoking. Try this statement: "Even though when I try to restrict my smoking I feel deprived, I accept these feelings."

3. Address and treat the "feelings in the now" around smoking.

This requires you to identify smoking problems that trigger other feelings.

- Identify problem times that trigger cravings/urges to smoke.
- How do you feel when you see other people smoking?
- How do you feel when you smell cigarettes?
- How often do you think/obsess about smoking?
- Using all your senses imagine yourself at your goal of quitting (really feel it, smell it, see it, etc.)
- Are you aware of how you feel in your body and mind when you smoke?
- How do you feel about yourself being a smoker?
- How would you feel if someone took away your cigarettes?
- Picture yourself with only one cigarette for the week. How do you feel?
- Picture yourself having half a cigarette and leaving the rest. How do you feel?
- Picture yourself throwing a whole packet of cigarettes away. How do you feel?
- Do you use smoking to reward yourself?

4. Address and treat the "past feelings and memories" around smoking.

Many habits are rooted in the past for us. Many clients talk about behaviors or specific smoking problems that are associated with particular memories, e.g., I used to smoke with dad at the pub after work. Do you have any?

- What events from the past make you feel anxious/guilty/ashamed?
- What traumas from the past are you numbing with cigarettes? When did you first smoke? What feelings were you trying to cover up?
- When did you first use or abuse cigarettes to alter your mood? Was it a positive or negative experience? Even positive first times can lead to wanting to recreate that in future smoking.
- What did your family or friends say the last time you tried to quit?
- What losses in the past did you smoke over?

  5. Address and treat "future feelings" around smoking.

What other future situations might trigger your urge to smoke? What other benefits are there to staying a smoker? What other costs or negatives are there to reaching and maintaining your goal? Who will be angry at you if you are successful? Who will be jealous of you or feel betrayed by your success? What other negative consequences will occur if you change your smoking habit? Are you afraid of leaving your comfort zone?

Explore all of these questions and tapping on the answers.

  6. Address and treat your lack of belief in your end goal success.

Picture yourself in the future at your goal (being a nonsmoker). How do you feel? Imagine yourself being somewhere and not able to smoke. Tap for any anxiety or discomfort that arises. Imagine yourself at a family gathering/work function and not smoking. Tap for any anxiety or discomfort. It is important to future-proof yourself too and tap on how you *think* you will cope.

A Final Note

Once you have tapped on any of the above ideas until your discomfort ratings are down to a 1 or 0, you can do a positive round to install some positive beliefs. Continue to do this after every section.

The setup statement might be something like: "Even though I have these limiting beliefs that have blocked my success and sabotaged me, I choose to let them go and be a nonsmoker, in control, safe, happy, and healthy."

Your reminder phrases could be:

Eyebrow: "my limiting, sabotaging beliefs"

Side of Eye: "I choose to easily embrace change."

Under eye: "I choose to be a nonsmoker."

Nose: "I choose to let this go."

Chin: "I choose more positive beliefs."

Collarbone: "I choose to be in control and happy."

Under arm: "I can be healthy, safe, and successful."

Top of Head: "I'm successful, happy, and healthy."

We know smoking raises blood pressure and increases blood clots, increasing the risk of stroke. But did you know that, as soon as one day after a person quits smoking, their blood pressure begins to drop, decreasing their risk of heart disease? This is the last area in this chapter for us to unpack.

Blood Pressure

By now I hope you are noticing how effective tapping is as a stress-reduction technique. Because of this, it has a profound ability to impact the body's physiological systems. In one of my own research studies,[6] 203 participants attended a four-day workshop to learn tapping in various locations. At one workshop 31 of them received comprehensive physiological testing. Not only did psychological improvements occur (significant declines in anxiety, depression, posttraumatic stress disorder, pain, and food cravings, and improvements in happiness), but significant improvements were found in resting heart rate, systolic and diastolic blood pressure, and cortisol readings. The whole study showed that tapping results in positive health effects as well as increased mental well-being.

Many studies have now shown that high blood pressure (or hypertension) increases the risk for cognitive issues, as well as dementia. In one study,[7] participants with high blood pressure were nearly three times as likely to experience cognitive decline when assessed after four years. While there are many ways to address blood pressure, both lifestyle and medical options, tapping may be used to address stress or anything contributing to the issue. This is not suggested to be a cure or the only strategy to use here; it is simply an additional technique to assist with contributing factors such as stress.

Sometimes simply addressing stress in your life with tapping can have a positive effect on blood pressure without you directly targeting it. And I highly recommend that this become a daily strategy. Here, however, is an approach you could take to precisely target high blood pressure (always seek medical advice if you are concerned about your blood pressure).

First, if you have high blood pressure, ask yourself how you feel about it. Is it something you deal with daily that is painful, annoying, frustrating, or burdensome? Can you take each of these feelings and tap to reduce their intensity?

When you first noticed the effects of higher blood pressure (this might have been symptoms such as headaches, anxiety, shortness of breath, nosebleeds, heart palpitations, or feeling of pulsations in the neck), what was happening in your life? Often someone is aware of these symptoms before they are actually diagnosed, and it is really about remembering when they *first started* (not when you were diagnosed). Thinking about any high stress that might have been happening at that same time or just prior could be a clue. It is worth doing some tapping (alone or with a practitioner) on those life events. If you find that stress is just difficult to cope with in general, then making tapping a daily practice can improve your ability to cope overall.

Of course, if you can't remember what contributed in the beginning, you can tap for this: "Even though I can't remember what was happening at the time my blood pressure started to increase, I am open to remembering."

Dr. Michael Valenti shares how he helps his patients and how asking when it started is very helpful.

* * *

I am a German general medical doctor and Master of Public Health. I have been using tapping for medical problems for several years. An interesting case of high blood pressure reveals the importance of always going back to the time when the illness started and demonstrates the obvious emotional background of hypertension.

Mr. C. came to me for a repeat prescription of blood pressure medication, because his doctor was on holiday. I saw the list of his four medications and asked: "Four tablets. That's a lot. How high is the pressure?" I checked the pressure and it was 220/140. "Oh, that's very high," I said. "I might have to send you to the hospital."

"No," replied the patient. "It's always like that." I asked: "Always, since when?"

The patient explained that he had had the high pressure of 220/140 for 20 years and that it never really went down, even with the medication. And that he would not go to the hospital, because they would just give him more useless medication.

So, I said: "Ok, let me try something."

I asked when the pressure problem had started, and he described how 20 years ago he had been working on a ship, had been called to the captain one day and told that his son was sick in Jamaica and that he had to fly home immediately. He had spent three weeks with his sick son in Jamaica, and after the son was improved, he had come back to the ship where his pressure was found to be very high. Since then, he was on the same medication, but the pressure never improved.

Based on this story I began to tap. I tapped three to four rounds on each of the following topics:

"Even though I was shocked when I was called to the captain and heard that my son was seriously ill...."

"Even though I felt guilty that I had not been there for my son...."

"Even though I have to work on the ship and I can't be there for my son...."

After these rounds, I checked the blood pressure and it was 140/90. I still prescribed the medication, since I didn't know if my treatment would last, but when I met the man in a bar two weeks later, he said the pressure was all right.

Many other cases of hypertension reveal similar relations to emotional issues that can be revealed by looking for stressful events in the client's life when the hypertension started—often relationship issues.

* * *

So, while every person will be different, the importance of asking yourself what was happening in life when your blood pressure first increased is vital. Reducing high blood pressure in general can impact cognitive functioning and protect against stroke and even dementia. I encourage you to make tapping a daily habit for stress in general in order to impact your physiology and memory!

Quick Action Steps

1. Take stock of the three topics we covered here: alcohol use, smoking, and blood pressure. If relevant, can you make it a priority to do some tapping this week?

2. Is there someone in your life who might benefit from knowing this information? Feel free to share the videos included on the website in case a loved one might be interested.

The next chapter shares some research and cases of where tapping has been used for more serious memory issues and disorders. While not suggested to be a way to prevent dementia or cognitive issues, tapping may still be useful for someone in the throes of these disorders as a calming strategy. The added benefit is that those who are carers of someone with dementia may find tapping very supportive in coping with their loved one.

CHAPTER 8

Cases of Tapping
for Memory Loss Disorders

The aim of this chapter is to share some cases of practitioners (and family members) who have used tapping with elderly people suffering the beginning phases or later diagnosis of memory loss disorders. While not intended to be a cure of any type for dementia or Alzheimer's disease, tapping has been used to alleviate other symptoms or early stages of memory loss. There has been some research conducted in brain injury areas, and I review what they found here as well. This is an important area in the research field, and I hope to witness more tapping research achieved in the coming years. I hope some of these cases are helpful if you have anyone in your life struggling with memory loss disorders. (Remember to seek the skills of a professional if you want to pursue tapping for anyone in your life who is suffering one of these disorders.) In this first case, EFT International certified practitioner Brenda Blair shares an experience of working with a woman in the early stages of Alzheimer's.

> What Is Dementia?
> Dementia is the loss of cognitive functioning and may include aspects related to thinking, remembering, and reasoning. It often also affects behavioral abilities to such an extent that it interferes with a person's daily life and activities (e.g., some cannot control their emotions, and for others their personalities may change). Many things may contribute to the development of dementia, and currently there are no cures.[1]

Early Stages

About seven years ago when I was living in Spain, I tapped with a lady in her early sixties who was in the early stages of Alzheimer's. She had become forgetful and had a rare form of it where her brain was

116

not sending the right signals to tell her body what to do. For example, when she went to pick up a cup, she couldn't get her hand in the right place to pick it up, or judge where the chair was when she went to sit, or change the television channel. And the hardest of all for her was that she was unable to do needlework, which was her passion. Over a number of sessions, we tapped on her frustration, anger, and sadness about what was happening, her anger at the lack of support for her and her husband from her children, on her fears of the future, her fears and embarrassment when it came to going out (e.g., going into a restroom she would get disoriented and wasn't able to find her way out again, or she was unable to feed herself properly in a restaurant).

And the biggest joy for her: They had a swimming pool. She loved to swim but was no longer able to dive into the pool, which meant she was dependent on her husband to lead her into the pool. We tapped away all the feelings and fears around that. The following week she was back diving into the pool unaided. I left Spain a couple of months later and she was still diving into the pool.

* * *

The joy in this case is the lady suffering the memory loss was able to engage in a much-loved pastime (swimming) and cope with the rare form of forgetting she was suffering. You may notice that Brenda was mostly tapping on emotions: frustration, anger, sadness, fear and embarrassment. By releasing those strong emotions, she appeared to also recover the ability for her brain to tell her body the instructions she needed (e.g., to pick up a cup). Tapping in the early stages of memory loss may be most beneficial when targeting the strong feelings someone has, as it is highly likely they are *aware* they have the memory loss. This is a disconcerting feeling: being aware that you can't remember. Research shows people rarely fabricate that they are having memory loss (the exception might be someone attempting to avoid a conviction as in a court case). Thus, if someone expresses worry about memory loss, then they will have feelings about this. They may benefit from using tapping to help calm their mind and body.

In this next case Sarajane Thomas, a tapping practitioner and volunteer in a hospice setting, shares a story of tapping with an advanced stage patient called Ruth. She discusses beginning with surrogate tapping in her presence (see box for an explanation) and

117

then taps directly on Ruth, who cannot tap herself. We would typically seek permission from a patient to tap on them, but, as you will read, Ruth appears to respond and want to actually tap herself. Sarajane was also a regular volunteer and the patients may have known her well and trusted her.

* * *

Dementia Diagnosis

Amongst other things that I do in my life, I'm a volunteer on a four-person hospice team that visits with dying patients at a nearby nursing home where they tend only to dementia patients. The current person [at the time of writing] I'm working with is a 78-year-old woman who had been ambulatory and able to feed herself up until about two weeks ago. She is diagnosed as being in the final/fourth stage of Alzheimer's disease.

I just got back from visiting with "Ruth." She is failing quickly at this time. When I arrived today for my visit with her, Ruth was falling asleep in a wheelchair in the dining room looking as though she were about to slip right out of her chair onto the floor. After two aides got her into bed where she would be more comfortable, I began singing softly to her and doing comfort touch on her right arm and forehead.

Since the tears that were quietly moving down her cheeks indicated she was in undue pain, I began to do surrogate EFT [tapping] work on her. I used the setup phrase, "Even though I, Ruth, am seriously ill, I deeply and completely accept myself." I could tell almost immediately that a part of her was somehow sensing what I was saying because her facial muscles began to relax and the pained expression was leaving her eyes. Furthermore, she was much more alert than before.

She lifted her head off the pillow, opened her eyes abnormally wide to look at me and kept them that way for the next half hour as though to say to me, "I know you're doing something I like." Then I began to actually tap very gently—with one finger—on her facial points. The distraught and pained expression on her face began to soften; she started to calm down. I just kept repeating the process again and again.

While absorbed in what we were doing together, I suddenly real-ized that she was responding even more to the tapping. When I would pause, she would actually lift her head up off the pillow in such a way that I could get to her face more easily, as though she were indicating she wanted me to continue. I kept on with the gentle tapping on her face again and again while I repeated to her in a whisper that she was seriously ill and very accepting of herself.

Later, I was even more amazed to comprehend that she was actu-ally trying to tap on herself. I sat there in wonderment and figured it just had to be an overactive imagination. However, I stayed in that calm place we had built together from the tapping, and I kept praising her as she struggled to make movement. One of her hands was close to the second point (on the side of the eye) and she could rub that spot easily, I noticed.

Even though I could sense that some deep part of her wanted to do the tapping for herself, the body just wasn't responding. And so, I took her hand, and as she would relax and allow me to do so, I would guide her index finger to the tapping points on her face. She was abso-lutely absorbed in what was going on. If she had been a kitten, I swear she would have been purring.

The hospice staff who supervises the volunteers feel that since a dementia patient has such a short attention span, the length of the visit should be limited to only 15 to 20 minutes. (I usually stay lon-ger anyhow.) I became so absorbed in what my friend and I were doing that after a while when I checked the clock, I found that I had been with her for over 75 minutes. As I prepared to leave Ruth for this visit, I could definitely tell she was still struggling to do the tapping. What a time to have to leave her. My heart so wanted to stay, but my train-ing was insisting that it was past time to leave. And, since we are required to report the time we spend with each patient ... [we ended the session].

This session with Ruth today was so intense that it would not have surprised me in the least if she had started to talk, something she has not done since I have known her these past three months. The biggest surprise of all today was that Ruth wanted to tap on her own behalf. I really look forward to seeing her again in another few days. In the meantime, I will be doing more surrogate work for her from my home.

* * *

Surrogate Tapping

In surrogate tapping, the practitioner taps on themselves as if they were the person whose problem is being addressed. This is done while holding the intention of helping that person. Similar to the distance version of reiki or other energy medicine approaches, there appears to be hundreds of successful reports of surrogate tapping in case studies.[2]

Debra Trojan shares in this next story how she assisted her own mother with tapping with the repeating questions one often gets from a patient. If you are trained in tapping but feel this is too close to home to tap with a parent, enlisting the professional skills of someone qualified is highly recommended, in order to allow you to stay in a different role.

* * *

Here's an EFT [tapping] success I've recently had with my 82-year-old mother who has Alzheimer's. She's been declining over a period of five years [at the time of writing]. She recognizes close family members but not friends. She can carry on a conversation as long as you keep it current. She's particularly deficient in her short-term memory. (After five minutes, she's forgotten what's she's done or said.)

She lives with my sister and her husband. Whenever they go on a trip, she stays with me. She can never remember where they are when they go. So, it's common for her to ask (very often) where they are.

A week ago, my sister and her husband went to Texas to visit their daughter. As expected, Mom started asking me where they were five minutes after settling in at my house. She continued to ask me where they were every few hours. Each time, I would tell her that "they flew to Texas to visit their daughter and their baby." After the fifth day (and after answering that question approximately 25 times), my frustration level was reaching a pinnacle. It's usually in times of frustration and desperation that I think of EFT. It occurred to me that if I tapped on her while I told her where they were, she might actually be able to remember it. (If only I had done this the first time she asked me.)

I had her repeat the phrase "they flew to Texas to visit their daughter and their baby" while I tapped on her. She was able to follow my lead on the 9 gamut [the original version of tapping had some eye

*movements in it] and really got into singing "Happy Birthday." I fin-
ished up with the sequence and waited 10 minutes before I popped the
big question. You can imagine how excited I was when, after reflecting
for a few seconds, she told me: "They flew to Texas to visit their daughter and their baby."*

*An hour later when my 16-year-old son came home from school, I
couldn't wait for him to ask her the question and see his surprise. Sure
enough, she delivered perfectly. Every couple of hours, I tested her. She
would always think for a few seconds and then come out with it. It's
been four days and she's still remembering. (I've asked her approximately 20 times in those four days.) Sometimes she has to think about
it, but (so far) she's been able to remember.*

*I'm speculating now that if I had tapped on her once or twice a
day since that first day, she probably wouldn't even hesitate when I
asked her. I'm now planning on experimenting more with her.*

* * *

Julia shares here about being a daughter with her father suffering
Parkinson's and then Lewy body dementia (a form of dementia that
occurs due to clumps of a protein in the brain). She primarily just
taps on the side of the hand point with him, but the outcomes are the
same: a calmness and sense of peace. The way her father describes
tapping is just perfect.

* * *

*My late father was diagnosed with Parkinson's disease in 2006. His
condition was relatively mild to begin with, and although there was a
physical deterioration over the years, it was slow. He was taking medication, which reduced tremors, but mentally he was still really with it.*

*Come late 2014, however, there was a marked physical change.
He was becoming a bit forgetful, but still keeping up with current
affairs. In October 2015 he started hallucinating, and then his mind
went—almost overnight.*

*He was taken to the hospital, where they treated him for a UTI
[urinary tract infection] and gradually took him off the Parkinson's
medication, as both the infection and the medication could have been
causing the hallucinations.*

*However, we later learned that the hallucinations and his mental
incapacity were caused by Lewy body dementia.*

When I arrived at the hospital, my father was in bed, agitated with all four limbs and his body uncontrollably writhing. He was not in pain—it was more like a nervous energy trying to get out of his body.

I sat on the opposite side of the bed to my mother, took my father's left hand in mine, put my thumb on the solar plexus point (reflexology) and began gently tapping on the karate chop point [side of the hand].

I continued to do this whilst Mum brought me up to date with what the doctors had said and done so far.

After a while, Mum told me to look as she pointed to Dad....

He had gone completely still, and was off in a deep sleep.

Around 10 minutes later, he woke up suddenly, rubbed his head, and looked around. His body was relaxed and still. Mentally, he was no longer able to take care of himself, but tapping literally "tapped" into a part of his brain that allowed him to communicate with me.

He was in the hospital for about eight weeks and was then moved into a nursing home, where it took a minimum of four hours driving round-trip for me to see him. Each time I visited my dad, I tapped on the karate chop point, nothing else. He told me things that were worrying him while I tapped. Whether they were long-suppressed memories, hallucinations, or things he had seen on the TV, I do not know. It brought him comfort.

I spoke with him by telephone every day. Some calls were bizarre, some amusing, some very upsetting. He always seemed to remember me and associated my voice, even over the phone, with safety. Clearly there was already a connection between us because we're family, but I am convinced that tapping made that connection deeper, allowing my father to continue communicating on a deep level when day-to-day interactions were beyond him.

For example, at Christmas, when I asked him if he wanted something to drink, he said, "Yes, something cool and in the shade." The nursing home was well heated, and Dad was telling us that he was too hot, but unable to say so directly.

I saw him again in early January, the weekend of my mother's birthday. Again, I did some tapping on the karate chop point. He was in good spirits that day and managed to sign a birthday card for my mother that I had brought with me.

When I telephoned him on the Sunday and Monday after, he kept asking when he was going to see me again. I wasn't planning to visit again that week, but he persisted and said he wanted to see me "for your soothing voice and thoughtful hands" and I thought, he wants me to tap on him again! I saw him that Wednesday, and when I tapped on his hand, it was as though he had a list of things to go through—things that were bothering him or had upset him. As I tapped, he spoke about it, and I reassured him—told him he had done the right thing—and then he'd move on to the next item.

He was in the moment, truly engaged in the memory or experience, talking in complete sentences, holding a conversation, whereas the rest of the time, he was off in a world of his own, often fixated on an idea. In early March of 2016, my father passed away peacefully. I thought my father's description of tapping as "soothing voice and thoughtful hands" was beautiful. It captures the technique perfectly.

I know that people with dementia are often anxious or seem to get stuck in a bad place mentally. Tapping seemed to allow my father to express his fears and move on, reducing his anxiety and bringing him some peace and calm.

* * *

Inherited Conditions

In this next case a tapping practitioner was referred a patient with Alzheimer's, where many members in his family had also suffered. While Dr. Debra Lohri had not worked with any patients like this before, and she didn't hold any expectations for spontaneous recovery. She was surprised at how tapping might have assisted Donny. Debra's orientation for this case was influenced by the work of Louise Hay, who documented common metaphysical contributions to illness and disease (note: this may not be appropriate or relevant to everyone suffering Alzheimer's). Some of the memories discussed below are also very serious forms of abuse, and while legal action was taken, please be mindful of your own reactions as reading (tap if you need to).

* * *

I recently had the opportunity to work with a patient with hereditary Alzheimer's disease. His father had it when he died, and a brother and sister are currently living with this condition. I didn't know quite what to expect since this was the first time in my six years of using EFT [tapping] that anyone with Alzheimer's disease had ever asked me for a session. I told the client—we will call him Donny—that I didn't know if it would help him, but I was willing to try.

I sat with Donny and asked him a few questions about if he remembered his childhood, and he said no, and I asked if there had been any traumas or accidents or anything else that may have contributed to the disease. He said he didn't remember. I asked his wife, who told me that there were in fact some traumatic childhood experiences. I knew from reading material in Louise Hay's books that Alzheimer's patients may be trying to block out an unsafe world and refusing to deal with it as it is, so that is where I began. As I wasn't able to take a SUD test, I decided to just tap on phrases that came to me about not being safe, not trusting the world.

I asked his wife if she had been aware of any painful memories that she believed were too mentally consuming and if she thought he had tried to block them out. She went on to explain to me a horrible generational story that started with his father. Apparently, his father was from a family where his father was not in the picture and the mother was raising several children on her own.

Financial burdens were so overwhelming on the single mother that she decided to prostitute not only herself, but also her older children. She believed the only way to keep custody of her children, be able to raise them on her own, and keep a roof over their heads and food in their stomachs was by selling them sexually for money.

So, Donny's father, being the oldest, was sent out to women, as well as to many men. He in turn grew up and started sexually abusing his own children. Although Donny was never part of the horrendous acts his father perpetrated on his older siblings, he was aware of what the five older children were going through and he would be tortured the rest of his life with those cries for help.

The father eventually went to jail for his violent offenses, where he died, leaving the older children to help with raising the younger children. This gave me a starting point to get tapping on. We started with "Even though these bad things happened to my brothers and sisters...." Remember, I couldn't ask him for a SUD level as he didn't even remember how to tie his shoes. In his fifties, he had already had this condition for three years. Five years is the average lifespan after official diagnosis and I understand that is with medication.

We then worked on:

"Even though I don't remember how to sign my name...."

"Even though my childhood is too painful to remember...."

"Even though my dad abandoned me and I never got to know him...."

"Even though Mother didn't know what Dad was doing to the other kids...."

"Even though I don't want to remember those bad memories...."

"Even though I am angry at my father for what he did...."

"Even though I feel angry at my mother for not protecting us...."

"Even though I feel ashamed at what happened to them...."

"Even though I feel sorry for them...."

Nothing else came to mind as I worked with Donny. I wasn't sure whether we had made any progress at all. It was hard to tell with someone who couldn't think clearly and answer questions. So, I blindly did the best I could. I really didn't expect much without his SUD ratings and given his inability to communicate.

That was on a Sunday morning in April 2009. I received a call from his wife on Monday morning with excitement and happiness. She told me that she'd had to talk to his doctor about some medicines he was taking and they told her that they couldn't discuss his medical treatments with her since she had not sent a power of attorney to the office for them to keep on file. She was really frustrated, as she already knew he would not be able to answer questions from the doctor or nurse on his own. His typical answer in our sessions was "I don't know." But his wife, not knowing what else to do, went ahead and put him on the phone to his doctor. They wanted to start by verifying his age and date of birth. She said he looked at her while talking to the doctor and answered, "August 15, 1956," and he then he said, "I'm 53." She said she couldn't believe he knew those answers. She said, "Donny, did you just tell them your age and birth date?" She was convinced it was the EFT, as all the medicines he had been taking gave him severe headaches, as well as made him seem a little "out of it" most of the time. For someone who couldn't even sign his name, this was astounding!

I was really excited with his small amount of progress. However temporary or permanent the changes, we didn't know. She didn't think to ask him again over a period of hours or days to see if he could still remember this information, but we can be sure that EFT did make some difference to his memory, even if it was short-lived.

* * *

The possibilities of assisting those with advanced forms of memory loss are endless. Even those who may not have the ability to speak, recall past events, or focus in the present still appear to respond to tapping. As mentioned earlier, I do hope to see more research conducted in these areas and clinical protocols developed. Before outlining some preliminary research that has been conducted, I wanted to share one last area where tapping can be of benefit here: for caregivers themselves. Compassion fatigue can occur for any caregiver. It is often thought of as the negative cost of caring: a condition where you may feel emotional and physical exhaustion and ultimately a diminished ability to empathize or feel compassion for others. Because caring can be demanding, draining, emotional, and personal (especially if caring is for a family member), it is not uncommon to see signs of compassion fatigue. These may include exhaustion, anger or irritability, a reduced ability to feel sympathy and empathy, a reduced sense of enjoyment or satisfaction with work, and even coping behaviors such as drug and alcohol use.[3] In this next case EFT International certified advanced EFT practitioner Carna Zacharias-Miller outlines caring for someone with dementia and working with a client who felt guilt over placing her partner in a nursing home.

* * *

Being the primary caregiver of a family member who has Alzheimer's or some other form of dementia is traumatic and demanding. There are many aspects to handle, for example: the tremendous emotional toll (loss of the established relationship with a spouse or parent, which brings up fear, anger, depression, and grief); administrative, legal, and financial issues; medical and physical problems; or dealing with other family members who can be either missing in action or meddling.

One of the most difficult decisions to make is at what point the transfer into a nursing or other care home is appropriate. Dementia is not a disease that gets worse in a linear fashion. There are days or moments when the patient is exactly the person we have known: sweet, connected, and completely clear in his or her mind. There just is not one obvious marker that indicates for everybody, without a doubt, when the time for a care home has come.

This leaves the primary caretaker who has to shoulder the full responsibility for another's life in an agonizing conflict: Am I really doing the right thing here?

"Miriam" came to me in order to work on all the aspects of the impending transfer of her life partner with Alzheimer's, "John," into a nursing home. The separation from somebody she had lived with on and off for 40 years, through good and also very bad times, seemed unbearable to her. It also stirred up other painful memories of separations from her parents, lovers, friends, and two of her siblings.

In one of our sessions, we worked specifically on the feeling of guilt about putting John in a nursing home. This guilt was experienced by her as pressure on the top of her head, and it had a lot to say. So, we tapped [side of hand setup statements]:

- *"Even though I am in this impossible situation that has no perfect solution, I do the best I can, and I am willing to accept myself."*
- *"Even though I have constant doubts about making the right decision, I treat myself with kindness and compassion."*
- *"Even though I have this piece of guilt wedged into my head, I soothe and comfort myself."*

We tapped through the points giving the guilt a voice:

- *"I am not letting you forget."*
- *"You are irresponsible."*
- *"I am not happy about how you are handling this."*
- *"I know everything, and you know nothing."*
- *"You are stupid."*
- *"I make the right decisions. You can't."*
- *"Only I do it right. You don't."*

I ended this sequence with a little re-frame, and Miriam laughed: "Not that an obnoxious little piece of guilt knows anything about making the right decisions."

The holding, grabbing sensation on top of her head was dissolving, and the piece of guilt said: "I'm melting, and I am not happy about that!"

Miriam described it now as a little bubble with a big mouth. "It is loud-mouthed, a know-it-all just sitting there and criticizing my every move. It is like a leech, feeding off itself, not helpful in any way." Since an energy form cannot just disappear, I asked Miriam what job we could give this piece of guilt that would actually be helpful. Miriam closed her eyes and envisioned that the big-mouthed bubble burst and its energy was transformed into a mass of tiny, sparkling stars that would help her make the right decisions.

"This is so beautiful!" Miriam said. "Twinkling stars dancing around my head and singing: 'We love you; we love you…'"

As mentioned, there are many tasks involved for the primary caretaker of a person with Alzheimer's dementia. If not handled well, they can lead to caretaker burnout, which is an emotional and phys-ical breakdown. When doing EFT either in a practitioner-client rela-tionship or working alone, it is crucial to get specific. A situation like this brings up everything of the caregiver's personal issues, from child-hood abandonment; the loss of other family members, lovers, and friends; old guilt feelings; and money fears to anxiety about the future. Also, spiritual questions might come up, like: "What is the meaning of all of this?" or even "Why is God doing this to us?"

There is no perfect solution; there are no easy answers. However, EFT can greatly ease the emotional pain, help solve problems, and advance the spiritual journey.

* * *

In this last section, tapping practitioner Jondi Whitis offers some insight into how we can approach taking care of ourselves as we care for others. She suggests entering into this tapping session with gladness that you can give of yourself to someone who gives wholly of themselves each day to another. Set your intention together to restore, strengthen, and find new springs or energy, resourceful-ness, peacefulness, and compassion within.

If you are currently caregiving in any role (even outside of dementia patients), tune in to how you feel right now. Rate out of 10 any emotion you may have. Substitute your exact feelings for those in bold below. Begin tapping on the side of the hand with these setup statements:

- "Even though I am weary and I there is no end to this in sight, I want to accept myself."
- "Even though I am so tired, and don't know if I can continue this way, I really do want to accept myself, and I'm doing the best that I can."

- "Even though I don't know how much more of this I
  can take, I accept that this is how I really feel, and some
  days that has to be enough. I want to accept myself even
  on days like this."

Tap through the eight points:
Eyebrow: "really exhausted"
Side of Eye: "It never lets up. It's overwhelming."
Under Eye: "What if it never lets up? It's never-ending."
Under Nose: "I'm so tired, so … I don't know how to keep going
when I feel this way."
Chin: "What if I can't? Then what?"
Collarbone: "It's terrifying to think I can't go on, but it's also ter-
rifying to think what if I can? Just because I can, does that mean I
have to? And for how long?"
Under Arm: "Is there any good end to this?"
Top of Head: "I'm exhausted."

If any of the statements above resonated, stay with them and
continue tapping. Check in with your SUDS out of 10. Here are more
setup statements you can try:

- "Even though I find it hard to keep going, is there any good
  end to this? I do accept myself. Most of the time, anyway."
- "Even though I am worried, what if I can't continue on this
  way? What if I have to? I really do want to accept myself, and
  this is the best I can do right now. I'm pretty sure that's the
  truth."
- "Even though I feel that if I ask for help or tell anyone how I'm
  feeling they'll think I'm a bad person, I accept that this is how
  I really feel. Don't I get to feel like being helped, too? I accept
  myself and this feeling."

Eyebrow: "Exhausted and guilty. Really? Hmm, maybe not guilty,
maybe just … alone and unhappy."
Side of Eye: "This tiredness that makes my brain hurt, that
makes me feel burnt-out. And why'd I ever think I'd be good at this?
Did I really have a choice? It's hard to tell anymore."
Under Eye: "What about me? Did I just say that?! What if that is
actually okay?"
Under Nose: "Maybe it's not my fault."

129

Chin: "Maybe it's not their fault, either. Maybe it's no one's fault. I'm just exhausted, that's all."

Collarbone: "Maybe I could just use a little break. Maybe I could use a little 'care,' too."

Under Arm: "Is it possible I could get help, too? That it's okay to ask? Who would I ask, anyway?"

Top of Head: "I don't know if I can go on this way, so tired and feeling guilty."

Again, check in as to how you feel and which statements resonate more. Continue tapping until a shift occurs or the SUDS rating is low.

Jondi says to now say out loud: "Even caregivers need care, I guess. How would that feel? Could I let that feel good?"

Here are some setup statements:

- "Even though I find it hard to ask for help, I accept myself. I really do."
- "Even though I'm supposed to be the caregiver, maybe I need care, too. And I really do want to feel better, like my old self. Maybe this is the best I can do right now, though. Maybe I really do accept me."
- "Even if I ask for help or tell anyone how I'm feeling and they won't listen, could that be okay just to try it? I accept that I feel nervous about saying this out loud, about asking for help."

Tap through the points:

Eyebrow: "Maybe I could reach out. Maybe no one actually knows what a toll this is taking on me."

Side of Eye: "What if they reject me? What if they say no? Is there anyone else I could talk to?"

Under Eye: "Maybe I need to say it to someone new. Maybe there's help out there for me I didn't know about."

Under Nose: "I don't know what I'm doing anymore, but I'm willing to admit I need some help here."

Chin: "I don't even know where to begin. I'm nervous about asking for help and being rejected."

Collarbone: "I'm nervous either way. What if they say 'Okay'? What if they don't?"

Under Arm: "Either way, I might feel better, just saying it out loud."

Top of Head: "Maybe I'm not a bad person to ask for help. Maybe it doesn't make me weak or look bad to ask for help."

If anything in the tapping sequence and ideas above resonates more with you that the rest, stick with those words. Keep tapping until you feel some change has occurred. Reach out for expert guidance if you need it (see Chapter 10).

The last section here is a brief summary of some research that has been done in areas related to memory loss conditions. An important area in dementia is that of sleep and insomnia (see Chapter 6). This is a common condition in the elderly and those with dementia, and a study is outlined below. But first let's look at some research related to brain injury, where electroencephalogram (EEG) monitoring during tapping sessions revealed increasing patterns of relaxation and centeredness as the treatment progressed. While this case is not classically a dementia one, many forms of brain injury can result in similar symptoms and may well lead to forms of dementia. Thus, resolving any issues to do with the precipitating event may be useful.

Research on Brain Injury

Clinician Gary Craig (and founder of EFT) describes the resolution in one session of several residual symptoms following severe traumatic brain injury six years earlier in a 51-year-old woman. Sally had been involved in a serious car accident and presented with poor balance (needing a walking stick), pressure in her head, and confusion. Sally described in her own words here what happened. Mind Mirror electroencephalograph (EEG) readings were collected during the single session (a type of neurofeedback hardware/software combination designed to measure specific brain waves reflecting various states of consciousness). As one deepens the relaxed and transformative state, one enters into a brain wave pattern characterized by increasing alpha and theta brain waves (such as when you fall asleep). Because tapping practitioners and clients always describe a state of calm, the researchers in the team were curious to measure this in real time.

Sally's Report[4]

It all started with a Thanksgiving vacation that never occurred. It was November 2001 and my family (husband, two children, and my parents) were driving from Connecticut to Florida to board a ship for a Caribbean cruise. Well, the trip came to an abrupt end with a horrific accident on Route 95 in Florence, South Carolina. Two vehicles rolled over without ever touching. They were just trying to avoid one another. The front-seat passenger in each vehicle perished in the rollovers. The drivers were pretty much untouched. There was a couple heading south in a small pickup truck and the six of us in our SUV. My mom, the driver, and my son were bruised; my dad perished; and my husband, daughter, and I were in intensive care with many complications. Thank the heavens above that we were near McLeod's, a great trauma hospital. I have no memories from two months before to a month after the incident; and I really and truly don't want to know all the things that were wrong with me and my body. I do know that I had lots of broken bones, collapsed lungs, a punctured bladder, broken hips, and my life was touch and go for quite a while. But the major long-lasting issue is my traumatic brain injury (TBI).

I don't remember anything from McLeod's hospital. I don't remember being upset about the loss of my dad. I have been told that when I was in the hospital, each time someone told me my dad died, I would get very, very upset and cry hysterically. Then, when I was distracted with something else, I wouldn't remember my dad had died until someone would tell me and it was like I heard it the first time and was out of control again. I've been told that it took months before I really understood and remembered that he was gone. I must have cried all my tears during those times. I don't remember the details because since I got home from rehabilitation I don't get upset about his loss. I just miss him.

Once the life-threatening problems passed, I was airlifted to Gaylord Rehabilitation Hospital in Connecticut. It is there I was re-taught to drink, eat, walk, and talk, with the aid of occupational therapy, physical therapy, speech therapy, and more. I continue to have to relearn things I think I remember how to do, yet I have to be shown because I just can't remember or figure them out when I go to do them. I only have a spotty memory of my time at Gaylord. The first thing I remember at Gaylord is the net bed I was zipped in, then the eating tests needed so I could graduate to eating bread and other foods, then the physical therapy with the walker, and on to walking using bars in the gym. I was told I always wanted to get out and go home.

I now go to a TBI support group once in a while, and the group leader has TBI and was hospitalized with TBI on the same floor as I was, when I was there. He told me I cried loudly all the time when I was a resident. This really surprises me, considering that I'm generally not a crier about anything. Traumatic brain injury has many facets and affects the individual in ways that are not easily visible. In my case, most are cognitive and short-term memory related. Yet my balance was gone due to injury to my left ear from the accident because I have a hole through my ear into my head.

Consequently, since I returned home, if I walked any distance or was in very challenging environments I really needed and used a walking stick. I was unstable walking, experiencing significant vertigo—feeling everything around me was spinning and that I would fall down if I didn't have the walking stick. It was a horrible feeling of insecurity and instability. These feelings really limited where, when, and how long I would go anywhere. My ear, nose, and throat (ENT) doctor said the physical reason I needed the walking stick was to compensate for the balance loss in my left ear.

When I speak of being in challenging environments, I mean places like stores, greenhouses, and surroundings with things near my head. Sometimes there wasn't anything we could see that would set me off. But it would happen all of a sudden and that's when I needed my walking stick or support of someone or of something and I had to get out of the environment immediately. My "head doctor" was working with me to get past this problem for several years with minimal progress. My ENT doctor said to keep using the walking stick and that many businesses have security systems on all the time and the electromagnetic fields could be negatively affecting me. He also said my balance will always be an issue due to my loss of my sense of balance in my left ear. He even did surgery to try and close up the hole internally, so he was basing his opinion not just on my symptoms but also on what he saw in the surgical procedure within my ear. So I thought I would just have to deal with the balance and vertigo issues the rest of my life.

Then I had the opportunity to spend a few days with Gary Craig, the founder of EFT and several other excellent EFT experts. It was then that I did EFT and got rid of the walking sticks for good. When I arrived at the facility where I met Gary Craig and the EFT'ers, I was OK until I walked down a hall that had patterned carpet that literally pushed me over the edge. I had my walking stick and I still needed to hold onto the

wall and vertigo was spiking through me. I found it unbearable. I liter-
ally could not take a step without holding onto the wall with one hand
and my walking stick with the other. Panic just filled my body as I felt
like I was weaving, spinning, and completely unstable. Then I had the
opportunity to experience EFT with the best therapists.

The focus of the EFT affirmations was on the balance and lack of
stability. It wasn't possible for me to relate this problem to an event
that seemed to have caused it since I can't remember before or after
the incident that created this situation. So we didn't tap on an event
with a crescendo of the problem because I didn't have any such focus
to relate to. So the tapping focused on the symptoms at hand at the
moment. When asked how I felt on that carpet area on a scale from 1
to 10 with 10 being the highest, I said it is definitely a level 10 of sever-
ity. I didn't think it could get any worse.

As we tapped about the feelings and the vertigo symptoms, the
severity started to subside. Several additional EFT rounds were done
that significantly reduced the severity. Then off to the patterned car-
peted area again. It was absolutely amazing and also hard to believe
that just minutes before I could barely stand to be on that carpeted
area and that now I was there without holding onto the wall, with-
out the walking stick, with no vertigo. It was incredible! I was able to
do jumping jacks, run in place, hop on one leg, and spin around. How
could that be? EFT was the only thing I did that could have brought
about these changes. I don't really understand it or question it. It was
great! Since then, still no walking stick.

Over a year has passed, and I don't get overcome with vertigo
symptoms like I did and don't need the walking stick. I haven't used it
once in 17 months since the EFT sessions that eliminated the problem.
I'm doing more and going more places with this issue lifted. I no longer
have to strategize where I'm going or how long I will be there like I did
before. My children loved going shopping with me before the accident,
but after the injury shopping was out of the question. Any shopping
during that time was for really short store visits (like minutes), and I
absolutely needed the walking stick. Now, since learning EFT, I go just
about anywhere with limited impact.

At times I get overwhelmed, resulting in a pressure in my head, yet
no more vertigo, and no more walking stick. I'm stable and feel reason-
ably balanced, not 100 percent but more than adequate. I feel so blessed.
As I mentioned, there are still times that I can feel pressure in my head

resulting from something in the environment, yet no vertigo or major balance issues occur. If I need to stay in the environment, I always have the option to use the EFT tapping to lessen the intensity of the symptoms. If it's uncomfortable doing so where I am at that moment, I can usually find a bathroom and I can go into a stall and tap the symptoms to a negligibly low level. So, my symptoms decreased from 100 percent every time when I went into retail environments to about five percent of the time.

It is just remarkable that tapping on a series of pressure points could relieve such symptoms not just at the moment, but into the future as well. No drugs, pills, only tapping on different points on the body combined with simple affirmations. This can even be done through a surrogate tapper as well, who taps on herself or himself in my place. I am forever grateful to Gary and the EFT experts for this astounding technique. I still live with TBI and permanent effects of the injury, effects that I've learned ways to deal with and compensate for. For example, I find myself not remembering things even after being told several times. I am easily fatigued, becoming overwhelmed and easily distracted. The things I used to excel in, like multitasking a large number of activities concurrently and accurately and understanding and retaining details are beyond my capabilities now, but that's ok. I take life less seriously and more spontaneously and simply.

I choose to look for the good in any situation and try to let the rest go. That's big for me. Being in the present and in peace is what I desire and where I want to be. Using EFT really helps when I notice I'm off track. I can use EFT to get myself back on track. And what's funny is when I might be getting off track my son even says, "Mom, tap, ... tap, tap." During the time with Gary Craig and others, many tests were conducted looking at my blood, brain waves, meridians, and other functions before and after EFT sessions. One thing that was clarified was the value of using the 9 gamut. This is a short process that uses both the right and left sides of the brain and gets them to work together effectively. There was definitely a difference noted in the brain wave test results when I did this. So when I do a round of EFT, I immediately follow up with a round of 9 gamut. It only takes a few more seconds and it really solidifies the results.

* * *

Sally's experience of the single tapping session was mirrored by her EEG state. First, the nonstop, chattery, "monkey mind" of high frequency beta waves (24 to 38 Hz) began to decrease in amplitude, while the lower frequencies of beta waves (13 to 20 Hz), present when there is less anxiety, increased proportionately. Second, an increase of the alpha/theta wave band (4 to 13 Hz) was observed. As Sally felt an improvement in her light and sound sensitivity and balance symptoms, her brain shifted. The researchers were also able to observe Sally the next day in this training and found her improvements were similar to the day before, consistently reflecting fewer stress and anxiety patterns, more left/right hemispheric balance, and more access to the subconscious mind (alpha and theta) without the challenges of anxiety or fear (too much high frequency beta) blocking her new behaviors and abilities.

At some level, tapping was able to re-organize Sally's nervous system that was severely damaged by physical trauma and positively impact her daily functioning and coping. Other tapping research has examined TBI caused during war situations and has found similar results.

In a 2016 study investigating subclinical post-traumatic stress disorder (PTSD) symptoms as a risk factor for a later diagnosis, 21 veterans were tracked to see if they developed the disorder.[5] Some received treatment as usual (TAU), and the other group received TAU plus six sessions of tapping. At the end of the program the TAU group were also offered the additional tapping sessions. For those who received tapping, they had a 64 percent reduction in their scores on a questionnaire indicating risk for PTSD, and they maintained this at three and six months later. The study also showed reductions in traumatic brain injury symptoms and insomnia.

Let's turn now to that other area of insomnia and how tapping can help.

Research on Insomnia in the Elderly

Sleep concerns in those diagnosed with a memory loss disorder can be difficult to manage. Medications are often used, and negative side effects of these are common. Tapping may be an option to assist with calming the mind and body in the elderly and those with these disorders. There has been a study conducted on 20 women over the age of 80 years who received either tapping or a sleep hygiene education program.[6] These were taught in groups, and eight one-hour sessions were delivered twice a week for four weeks. Members of the tapping group were also instructed to self-apply tapping via the use of a cassette tape and recorder and asked to listen and follow instructions at least once per day. They were all assessed for insomnia severity, depression, anxiety, and life-satisfaction before and after treatment. The tapping group had superior outcomes to the sleep hygiene group for insomnia (although not for anxiety or life satisfaction).

While this study was not specifically targeted at dementia patients, the benefit may be there nevertheless. Loss of sleep in the elderly has been tied to loss of memory, decreased concentration, and decreased functional performance in daily activities. As mentioned in Chapter 6, an improvement to sleep patterns may positively affect other areas in life, including memory.

* * *

Quick Action Steps

1. Pause for a moment and reflect on which story may have had the most impact here. Is there anything relevant in these cases you can take into your own life or share with someone who is currently a caregiver? Chapter 10 outlines further resources and referrals if you would like to pass this on.

The next two chapters will outline a complete tapping plan and also answer all your questions. I hold a vision that everyone will learn tapping and be able to calm their mind and body at the snap of a finger (literally). While you may be new to tapping from this book and not yet ready to share with anyone until you have results, it is vital to have a plan to achieve this! Therefore, I give you a practical plan, a way to ponder your own life and use tapping to resolve or release any issues that still cause some bother. So, let's head into that; have a pen and paper ready.

CHAPTER 9

A Tapping Plan for Life

Having spent more than a decade conducting clinical trials with tapping (for a range of conditions), I know that the outcomes last a long time. Many of our participants engage in tapping for the eight-week trials but then move on, never to tap again! (We do ask them in our follow-up surveys.) It's almost as if they get their outcomes and forget to return to this fantastic stress-reduction technique.

My wish for you, the reader, is that if you have given tapping a go throughout this book, and had some outcomes, that you will keep tapping!

This tapping plan for life is designed for just that. You may venture outside of tapping for memory issues and start using it next time you feel really tired and just need that caffeine hit at 3 p.m. You might have a fight with your partner and still feel angry hours later but use tapping to calm down. You might also remind your children to tap when they feel overwhelmed with their homework. Tapping can be applied to any emotion, anywhere and anytime.

I first want to share five ways to soften the tapping setup statement by Betty Moore-Hafter. These gentle applications can help with even the most persistent issue. Now that you know how to apply tapping, you can start to adjust the recipe.

* * *

I believe the EFT setup statement paves the way for healing, shifting the hard, locked-up energy of fear to the softer energy of self-acceptance. I have found that creative wording with the setup phrase can be especially helpful toward this end. Here are five of my favorite ways to soften the EFT setup statement:

1. ***With kindness and compassion: "Without judgment."***

These and similar words added to the setup contribute an extra dimension of support and care. Especially when the issue is a sensitive one, tears often come to people's eyes as we add these simple words. Here are some examples:

- *"Even though I feel unworthy, I deeply and completely accept myself with kindness and compassion."*
- *"Even though I'm so afraid of rejection, I deeply accept myself with gentleness and compassion."*
- *"Even though I feel guilty for that mistake I made, I totally accept myself without judgment."*

I have experienced firsthand how good it feels to hear these kind words—and how much emotion they bring up. For me, they speak right to the heart.

2. Welcoming: "I want to bring healing to this."

Some people balk at the words, "I deeply accept myself" and say, "But I don't accept myself! I hate myself for this."

One gentle way to proceed is this: "Even though I don't accept myself, I can accept that this is just where I am right now. And even though I don't accept myself, I want to bring healing to this. I would like to feel better, find more peace, reach more self-acceptance."

Whenever self-acceptance is difficult, just stating the intent for healing breaks the deadlock of self-rejection. Most people do want to heal and feel better.

3. The truth is: "I'm willing to see it differently."

These words can usher in powerful reframes. And when you reframe a situation while tapping, it does shift the energy and things begin to change.

- *"Even though I crave this cigarette, the truth is, cigarettes are making me sick."*
- *"Even though I still feel guilty, the truth is, I've done nothing wrong. This is false guilt."*
- *"Even though I still feel responsible for my sister, the truth is, she is an adult. She's responsible for herself now."*

Sometimes amazing things happen after adding the words "I'm willing to see it differently." One of my clients was convinced that she could never have a child because she might abandon that child like her father abandoned her. As we tapped through her pain from the father issue, I added the phrase "and I'm willing to see it differently": "Even though my father really hurt me, I love and accept myself, and I'm willing to see it differently."

After several rounds of tapping, she seemed calm and said thoughtfully, "You know, I think my father really did love me in his own way. That's all he was capable of." She felt at peace with it for the first time. And, when I heard from her later, she and her husband were talking about having children. She knew she was not her father and would do it differently. She saw it all differently.

With the above, I often tap the points in an alternating manner. Beginning on eyebrow, "still feel guilty." Side of eye, "But the truth is (etc.)."

4. ***Gain perspective: "That was then and this is now."***
When childhood pain is being healed, people often feel great relief when words like these are added:

- *"Even though when I was eight, I cried alone and no one came, I deeply love and accept my young self. And that was then and this is now. Now I have lots of help and support."*
- *"Even though I still feel anxious, afraid that something bad will happen, I deeply accept myself. And even though my child self felt anxious all the time, afraid my father would explode, I love and accept that child self. That was then and this is now. Now I'm safe. I don't need this hypervigilance anymore. I can relax now."*

5. ***Remaining open: "I'm willing to entertain the possibility."***
"Choice" statements are of course very empowering when we are ready for them. But sometimes stating a choice is too much of a stretch. Often, the gentlest way to introduce a better choice is to simply bring in the idea of possibility.

- *"Even though I'm full of doubt that I can lose weight, I deeply and completely accept myself and I'm open to the possibility that it may be easier than I think."*
- *"Even though I'm stuck in this anger and don't want to let it go, I'm open to the possibility that it would be nice to feel more peaceful about this."*

- *"Even though I don't think EFT will work for me, I deeply and completely accept myself and I'm willing to entertain the possibility that maybe EFT will help. I'm ready for some help."*

I believe that when we open the door of possibility just a crack, it is enough to set the healing process in motion. Experiment and see what works for you!

* * *

And with those extra tips in mind, let's turn to a plan that will keep you going for life.

Tapping Plan Tip #1

Tap Daily.

One of the ways to keep tapping in your life is to get into a regular routine. We recommend just five to 10 minutes per day and at the same time each day. You might choose first thing in the morning, when you are having your morning coffee (tap on how you slept the previous night or any feelings of fatigue). Or last thing at night when everyone is getting ready for bed, you tap on the day and anything you still feel about whatever happened. The main reason for tapping daily for five minutes is to establish a habit. If you are used to tapping for little things, you will more easily remember to tap when something bigger happens. Too often I hear people say, "That tapping was great. I will use it next time I feel really stressed."

But next time they are really stressed, they forget! If you commit to tapping daily on anything at all, it will become a habit that is easy to remember to do when you next need it most.

Tapping Plan Tip #2

Tap and Breathe.

If daily tapping sounds like too much too soon, perhaps commit to just using tap and breathe when you feel triggered by something in your life. If you feel your body tense after a stressful event, or tight after a restless night of sleep, use tapping on these physical sensations. Your body is a barometer, and you can think of it as a smoke detector.

If you feel stressed or overwhelmed, your body will likely feel tight, heavy, contracted, or tense. See these signs as just that—a sign your body needs some assistance to relax and unwind. You can just tap on those sensations when they are present in your life and start the process of reducing cortisol and introducing the feeling of calm. I know of friends who walk daily and tap as they walk—on anything that has happened in the day or week. You can tap before bed, just for five minutes, on any physical feelings and muscle tension. You will build a habit and at the same time positively affect your physiology!

Tapping Plan Tip #3

Keep a journal of what you tap on.

The benefits of writing in a journal have actually been studied. Just keeping a diary or journal has been shown to make therapy more effective for symptoms of depression, self-esteem, anxiety, panic, substance abuse, post-traumatic stress disorder, asthma, arthritis, and many other health conditions and disorders. The benefits to your physical health include improved blood pressure and immune system function, better sleep, and more buoyant mood.

There is a really important reason to keep a journal of what you tap on. It helps to keep track of what changes happen in your life because of tapping. Reading back over your journal in the weeks to come will show you how your tapping practice has worked. There is something in tapping called the "apex effect." This is where someone taps and then discounts that it was the tapping that produced the positive effects they experience in the coming weeks! We know through our long-term follow-up clinical trials that when something is not a problem anymore, how someone overcame it gets "forgotten" as well.

Here's an example from Dr. Silvia Hartmann, hypnotist and tapping pioneer.

One of the many people I helped with tapping was the proprietor of a New Age shop in my town. I walked into this shop one day, full of the joys of spring, and she was suffering from a severe neck-ache from having sat on a hard stool all day long, on a rainy day in late autumn.

She put the SUD level of intensity for her neck and back pain at an 8 to 9 out of 10.

We tapped one round. I didn't even get as far as the 9 gamut [included in older versions of tapping—a sequence of eye movements and fingernail tapping] when she started to giggle, then laugh, and the pain had gone completely—a "one-minute wonder," as it is called. I expected her to jump off the stool and have me tell her all about tapping, but she insisted I had just made her laugh and cheered her up and didn't want to hear at all about this new thing I was so excited about. She was patient, however, and even said that I could come in and do a demonstration at the shop on a busier Saturday weekend.

The demonstration was an amazing experience. I treated all sorts of people for all kinds of things, including virtually lifelong phobias, depression, and a fear of driving, and people were excited and delighted—apart from the shop owner, that is. She still wasn't interested in tapping at all beyond mere politeness and humoring me in a friendly enough fashion.

Then, a year later, I received a telephone call from that very shop owner. It seems, about a week prior to the call she had woken in the night with sincere menstrual cramps and "it just occurred to her from nowhere to tap for them." She did just one round of tapping and "they just disappeared into nowhere." Apparently, she sat in the bed and could not believe what had happened, and also, all of a sudden could remember all the things I had said to her in my desperate efforts to convince her, and all the miraculous things she had witnessed with her own eyes at the time, yet somehow failed to take in.

I struggled with myself whilst listening to her and then asked her if it was okay to briefly scream down the phone, "I told you so!" to get that over with.

It is also a sign to me and a hope that many other of the people who walk away from an introduction evening, a treatment session, or a friend showing them tapping over coffee and simply seem to forget what they saw, heard, and felt, will at one point or another remember, use the technique, and have their very own "Aha!" experience.

* * *

This apex effect happens when I check in with participants in our trials who have used tapping to reduce the desire for unhealthy foods (that contribute to a weight problem). I ask them one and two years later how their relationship is with the food they tapped on, e.g., chocolate (the most common one!). They typically say, "Oh, I

143

don't eat chocolate." I remind them that they used to eat a lot of it and show them the record they completed two years earlier. They usually laugh nervously and say, "I sort of remember I ate it, but I haven't even thought about it since the trial—I'm not sure why." I too want to yell—because you tapped on it!

Back to the journal! If you keep a record of what you tapped on and check back weeks and months later, it will help you discover if there is anything else left to tap on (perhaps a minor aspect) or you will remark, "I don't remember writing that, it doesn't bother me anymore!" My own husband did this recently. He has a tapping journal and was flicking back and said, "I don't remember writing this stuff. It [the issue] doesn't even feel like me anymore." It was in his own handwriting!

Tapping Plan Tip #4

Do a personal peace procedure.

This process came from the founder of EFT, Gary Craig. There were other versions of tapping prior to Craig's version we use now, but he was the one to propose this idea. Here are the steps:

1. Make a list of every event that has happened to you so far in your life that you wish had *never happened*. Try to write as many as you can (e.g., aim for 100 events).

2. Beside each event, rate the intensity or how you feel about each event from 0 to 10. Ten would be the worst, and 0 would be completely calm.

3. You can start wherever you like—choose the highest numbered ones first or a different number—but every day tap on one of them (use your journal to record your progress).

4. If you have created your list but do not find yourself tapping on any of the events and procrastinating, perhaps start tapping on just that. "Even though I find this list overwhelming … I accept this is how I feel."

5. After an event is a 0 in SUDS, cross it off the list and check the rest of the list. If you become aware of other events, add them to your list and rate them.

6. Every five events or so, go back through your list and re-evaluate the intensity ratings for each item. You might find some

of the lower numbered events don't rate as high now. This is called generalization and happens because they were related to the ones you have tapped on.

7. If you clear one event per day for six months you will have resolved 180 events!

8. If an event you listed feels too overwhelming to tap on by yourself, seek a practitioner to support you in the process.

Tapping Plan Tip #5

Do a 21-day challenge.

Start this week with a 21-day challenge! Below are some areas in life where you may like to use tapping. You could set goals in those areas and tap on them, or you might address things you are unhappy with. Tap daily and chip away at the topic areas. It might take longer than 21 days for tapping to become a habit (research suggests it actually takes 66 days on average for a new behavior to stick), but it will get you started.

Areas in life to consider for your 21-day challenge:

1. spirituality/knowing yourself/your life purpose
2. personal growth/learning/study/memory
3. family
4. friends/social relationships
5. physical health/fitness
6. emotional health/self care
7. career/business/work
8. fun
9. community/volunteer work
10. partner/love/romantic or intimate relationships
11. money/finance

Bonus Tapping Plan Tip

Try imagining tapping.

German researchers have done several studies where participants were put inside an MRI machine, and, rather than actually tapping on the acupoints, they imagined tapping. They did this while looking at images on a headset that created certain negative feelings. When they imagined tapping on those feelings, their ratings out of 10 still decreased, and their brain images reflected changes as though they were actually tapping.

What this means is that you can imagine tapping at times when it is inconvenient and still achieve the outcomes. An example would be when you are lying in bed at night, wide awake. You may not want to physically tap as it might stimulate you to wake up (or a bed partner next to you might wake up!). You could imagine tapping instead while you repeat the reminder phrases in your mind, and it will still work.

A Plan for Children and Teens

When parents ask me how they can encourage their children to tap, I usually ask if they are tapping themselves. It is important if you are a parent to be doing the very thing you want your children to do as well. Tapping can look unusual when it is new, and it is much easier to suggest it as a technique if you are using it too. When a child sees a parent tapping and then also witnesses you becoming calmer, they will associate the two! I do suggest parents openly tap (e.g., in the kitchen or lounge area of the house) so your family sees you. This makes tapping seem "normal" and again shows you are using it yourself. Of course, you may want to tap quietly and not out loud, particularly if you are tapping on feelings about people in your family! It is much easier to offer tapping as a way to achieve calm, feel better, and release other negative feelings such as anger when it is a common technique used by parents.

If you have younger children, you may like to have a bear or puppet on which to demonstrate tapping and then offer tapping during everyday activities such as going to bed to relax or at the start or end of the school day. I know parents who tap while driving to school— sometimes on the chaos in the morning rush, and sometimes just on having a great day today. Others tap at the end of the day on the drive home, on anything that happened (talk and tap works well here—no setup statement needed, just talk and tap at the same time). You can offer tapping during learning processes as Chapter 4 outlined, and even teach them discreet tapping for school situations.

Teens respond well to goal setting and using tapping to achieve something they really want, and this may be a good bridge to build when sharing tapping. Again, they would have seen you tapping at home anyway but not know you can use it to set goals. As described in Chapter 4, the best way to do this is to write a goal, then rate your level of belief it will come true and your level of doubt that it won't. Then you can tap for both areas separately. Keep reading the goal out loud to see if the belief increases and the doubt decreases. Tailenders (the little voice inside your head) that suggest the goal won't come true can also be targeted in a setup statement (e.g., "Even though my mind says there is no way this goal can come true, because... I accept that this is how I am feeling").

Of course, your teens may also be open to tapping on their emotions, stress levels, sleep patterns, peer issues, and more. If they are not open at all and perhaps think tapping is the dumbest thing they have ever seen, I suggest parents do this next step. You can also do this step if you want someone else to use tapping in your life and they won't (e.g., a partner, spouse, parent, best friend).

Ask yourself how you feel about someone else in your life who won't use tapping. If they reject it, ridicule it, and/or avoid it, how does this make you feel? Write down everything that comes up for you when you think about them not tapping.

I recommend you tap on this for yourself so that you don't have any desperate emotion around needing your children (or parents or spouse!) to use tapping. Tap on why you want them to tap and how you feel when they won't. You may find this helps you feel calmer, and they may become more open.

Summary of Tapping Ideas for Children and Teens

To improve memory try tapping on:

- spelling and other learning activities (e.g., times tables)
- when there is a test or exam looming and your child is worried about remembering what they studied (also teach the discreet tapping to use during the test)
- new languages (tap while saying the new words/phrases out loud)

- learning a speech
- beliefs about memory (do they believe they have a good memory or a poor one?)

Also try tapping on these general areas in life with your child/ teen:

- feelings of stress and worry
- other uncomfortable feelings (anger, hurt, embarrassment)
- how the day went at school
- peer and friendship issues
- teacher issues
- subjects that are disliked at school
- sporting success and goals
- self-esteem and confidence issues
- sleep issues
- resisting technology (!)

A Final Thought

Tapping works when you do it. When I hear someone say that tapping doesn't work I usually ask how often they tap. And they are very honest in saying—never! I'm not sure anything works if you don't do it.

Remember that lack of progress might mean you are being too global with your tapping statements and not being specific enough. It might also mean you need to consult with a trained practitioner for some guidance. The end of the book offers ways to find someone in your area.

My wish at the beginning of this chapter was that tapping would become a habit for you and perhaps even that the apex effect would happen. If you forget something actually used to bother you (because it doesn't any longer), then I have achieved my mission!

Tapping can and will support your memory. It will help your children learn and recall more effectively. It will reduce your stress levels and those of others with whom you interact. You will have the ability to turn off the stress response as fast as using your fingertips to tap on those acupoints. You can even explore childhood issues with a trained practitioner and resolve long-held hurt and distress.

Tapping is well supported by the science and research. As of 2022, there are more than 300 published trials showing its effectiveness and ability to last over time. A range of emotional, psychological, and physical issues have been explored. A colleague once said EFT should stand for "every feeling and thought"—because you can literally apply it to all of them! I guess you can.

If you have a question you want answered, the next chapter may contain it! I have included the most common questions asked once one knows as much as you do by this section of the book. If you are wondering where you should go now, and how can you find a trained practitioner, then Chapter 10 offers that as well. There is also a list of leaders in the tapping world and research sites to explore.

I hope this plan will get you started and well on the road to becoming a tapper. The applications are truly endless.

CHAPTER 10

Tapping Explained

By the time you have read this far, you may have some questions coming to mind. Perhaps you dipped in here along the way. Below are the most common questions people ask about tapping. If something is not covered here, you can reach out through the details at the end. I have also included some giants in the tapping world you may wish to follow as well. There is a wealth of knowledge and experience in these leaders, and they all have unique perspectives on tapping.

Finally, if you are seeking to dive deeper or enlist the services of a professional practitioner to continue your journey, you will find a way to do that at the end of this chapter.

Frequently Asked Questions About Tapping If You Are Starting Out

Q: How soon can I tap on my own?

You can use the technique on your own as soon as you understand the concepts in this book. There's no need to delay using the technique. Always know, however, that you can seek the assistance and support of professional practitioners, too.

Q: I have been reluctant to use the technique because I might get the setup or the tapping wrong. Does tapping have to be done precisely and perfectly?

No, there is no such thing as perfect tapping. For example, people with significant brain injury have reported benefits from doing their version of tapping that differed somewhat from what they were taught.[1] They were able to grasp the concept of tapping and gain benefits from the way they did it. If you are really worried about getting it right (and without the help of a professional), tap with the following setup statement: "Even though I am worried about getting the words wrong, and it might not work, I accept myself anyway" (the reminder phrase would be "worried").

Q: Can I make things worse if I don't do it exactly as taught?

No, you won't make anything worse—just stick to the basic recipe. If you don't feel you completed the process (e.g., by reaching a SUDS of 0 or 1), return to it another time. It is always best to tap until you feel calm or there may still be aspects to deal with. We also recommend that you seek the support of a certified tapping practitioner if you do need assistance.

Q: I don't seem to be able to say a number for my level of concern/distress. What do I do if I can't put a number on it?

We usually ask someone to rate their level of intensity out of 10 when tapping. This is based on Wolpe's 1960's SUDS scale (subjective units of distress), which is very commonly used in many therapies and validated to match your internal experience. However, not everyone likes numbers!

If you "tune in" to your body while tapping, you might be able to notice a sensation or feeling is less or more. You might also notice physical changes indicating that the tapping is working—e.g., people yawn, sigh, laugh, and the issue seems more distant/less intense in your mind's eye—these are all signs tapping is working too. So feel free to explore these other ways of "knowing." As a last thought, you can always tap on the following: "Even though I can't really rate my concern out of 10 and I don't know why...."

Q: I'm not sure I'm tapping in the right places. Will it matter if I don't get the exact point?

No, don't be concerned about getting the exact point. Using two or more fingers may give a better coverage of the points. You can also purchase an acupoint detector or pen that measures electrical resistance of the skin to accurately locate acupuncture points of the human body. When you scan the acupoint spots with such a pen, it emits an acoustic signal to indicate the exact location. This technique enables even lay people to locate the relevant points.

Q: If I miss a point will it affect the round?

No, you won't affect the round if you miss a point every now and then.

Q: Should I go back and tap on the missed point?

Yes, you can go back to a missed point and tap on it if you want. However, as you have read, children often only tap with four points out of the eight adults use, and it is still effective.

Q: I find some of the acupoints sore and tender. What do I do?

When acupoints are sore or tender, you can either gently touch them without tapping as such.

Just touching gently will still activate the acupoints. Alternatively, you can actually imagine tapping them in your mind (the brain still engages like you are doing real tapping). As long as you keep focusing on the reminder phrase as you imagine, it will still work. As mentioned earlier, German research in 2020[2] showed that imagining tapping still activates the acupoints.

Q: Do I have to use the same reminder phrase for each point in a round?

It helps to use the same phrase when you begin using the technique and for the first few rounds, but as soon as you feel some confidence you can change the reminder phrase. Go with the new thought/feeling if one comes up or use words that are similar to each other.

Q: How do I know what feeling to tap for?

Whatever the main unwanted feeling is in that moment is the one you set up and tap for.

Q: Can I swap hands when tapping?

Yes, you can use either hand, or even both. Some people, including children, like to use both hands while tapping—so both sides of the face/body are tapped at the same time. You don't have to do this, though. All the research trials only use one side of the body.

Q: What if there are so many feelings that I just feel confused or overwhelmed?

Rate, set up, and tap for feeling confused or overwhelmed. Just start there.

Q: What do I do if while I'm tapping a different strong feeling (maybe associated with a thought or memory) comes up?

Finish the round for the setup statement you started. Then immediately rate the new feeling/memory/thought, do a setup, and tap for that. The way to tap for a memory is outlined in the movie technique in Chapter 2.

Q: Sometimes I want to instinctively close my eyes when tapping. I know, however, that it might be better to keep them open. What should I do?

While it is okay to close your eyes to tune into what is happening for you (internally) if you are tapping alone, if any intense distress comes up, you may be better to keep your eyes open in order to stay grounded in the here and now. This prevents you from being swamped by emotion and feeling as though you are back in a memory that was very distressing. In therapy settings we ask clients to keep eyes open to help them stay grounded and present in the room with us and not be overwhelmed by past distress, which can happen if you are tapping with eyes closed. If you do feel overwhelmed, reach out to be connected with an experienced practitioner to help support you.

Q: If I'm in a situation that I feel uncomfortable saying the setup and reminder phrases aloud, can I say them to myself?

Yes, this still works. If you find yourself drifting and not staying focused, you may wish to continue at another time when you can say it out loud again.

Q: If I'm in a situation that I feel embarrassed/uncomfortable tapping, what should I do?

You can tap inconspicuously on any points you can and leave the others until you have the opportunity to tap in private. See the discreet tapping techniques for other ways to tap in public. Also, consider tapping on the feeling of being embarrassed/uncomfortable in the situations concerned.

Q: If I don't have a particular feeling and I say the setup and tap with someone who does, will that give me the unwanted feeling?

No, you won't take on someone else's discomfort. Tapping with someone else for his or her discomfort can give you an awareness of a similar aspect that you may have. In that way you may get "borrowed benefits" from tapping with them and reduce your own discomfort.

Q: Can I do tapping for someone else (e.g., my child who is too young to tap)?

Yes, this is called surrogate tapping, and it is where someone taps for another person while holding the intention of helping that person. It is similar to distance versions of reiki. There appear to be hundreds of cases of this being successful, although it has not been subject to clinical trials in tapping.[3] We do advise that this is not a substitute for someone using tapping themselves if they are able and not a way to change other people's behavior for your own gain.

Q: I have been tapping for a long time, and nothing is changing. What do I do now?

There are several things you can do. You could seek the services of an objective practitioner who can guide you. Sometimes when we tap alone, we stay too general and are not specific enough. A practitioner can assist with this. Another question to ask yourself is: Is there any reason I would not want this issue to change? Sometimes there are valid (although subconscious) reasons we don't actually want to change. If you ask yourself what will change in your life if the behavior or pattern in question does, you may find something there to tap on!

Q: I have something I want to tap on. Can I tap gradually over a few days rather than in one sitting?

Absolutely! Sometimes we run out of time, get tired, get over it … and need to stop. Honor yourself and take your time. We often recommend using a boxing up technique if you have not quite finished and want to come back to the topic/tapping later.

For whatever reason, you can always lock all of your worries or "stuff" into an imaginary box. How would you describe your box? Is it old or new? Covered in cobwebs? Does it have a lock on it? A padlock? What color is it? Does it have a smell? What does it sound like? How big is it? Where is it stored? Remember if the box gets too full with "stuff" you can always make the box bigger. Make sure the box is outside of yourself. It can even be in another room, in the garage, another country, etc.

Tap at the end of a session when you haven't yet reached a state of calm, or whenever you start to feel overwhelmed like this:

"Even though I have this box and it's full of [emotions], it looks like … , smells like … , it's stored … , I don't want to look at it, open it, or pay attention to it right now. But right here, right now I am safe/will be OK."

Now tap through the points:

Eyebrow: "Everything is in the box now."

Side of Eye: "This box that smells/sounds like..."

Under Eye: "This box filled with emotions of..."

Under Nose: "This box that's stored..."

Chin: "I am closing the lid tight."

Collarbone: "I don't have to look at this box or what's inside it."

Under Arm: "I can come back to it when I'm ready."

Top of Head: "Everything is inside the box, and I am safe right here right now."

And come back to it later when you are ready.

Q: I tapped on an issue and it seemed to be 0 out of 10. Then a week later it seemed to come back. Does this mean tapping didn't work?

This may look like tapping hasn't worked, but it may also mean that a different aspect is what comes back a few days later, something you may not have tapped on in the first instance. It is worth checking to see if there is a different feeling, a layer, a thought of something else when you check the issue later on. That is usually what is happening. It's not quite the same as the first time you tapped. Always remember to reach out to a skilled practitioner if you need assistance. With more than 300 clinical trials and years of research, we know tapping works. Sometimes a fresh set of eyes can help you uncover what is going on.

Q: Can I tap on more than one issue in the same sitting?

Yes, anything can be tapped on in one sitting as such. If thoughts/ideas seem to be different, though, it is always best to use a new and different setup statement. If you have time and energy, keep tapping!

Q: I have seen videos where someone does the setup statement once and then starts tapping, and others do it three times as per the original recipe. Does it matter?

With such a wealth of information available online these days there is a lot to choose from—even with tapping! The setup statement has its roots in two schools of psychology: cognitive therapy and exposure therapy. Saying your problem/distress/issue out loud (the cognitive part) is also helping you acknowledge what is happening and serves as the exposure part.

Often if you know the exact feeling going on for you and you want to tap to reduce it, you can start without a setup statement—just start tapping. With children we often do this and skip the setup statement. But if you were trying to work out what was happening for yourself, the setup statement helps you tune in and get focused (so three times might be better). The fact that you are tapping is the real winner here!

If you have a question that hasn't been answered in this chapter, always feel free to reach out via my website. These are the most common ones asked, but sometimes you might have others. There are a range of other resources to support your journey from here as well, and below is a list of tapping giants in the world who all offer a wealth of experience and information.

Tools to Support Your Journey

In 2019 one of my own dreams came true: I presented the topic of tapping at a TEDx event. It is on the official TED website and is called "Is Therapy Facing a Revolution?"

This is a great presentation to share with anyone new to the technique and gives the reasons why EFT tapping may be considered the fourth wave in the therapy space.

Over at the webpage for this book (*www.petastapleton.com/ memorybook*) you will find a range of resources to help you continue your journey. There are tapping worksheets for children and teens, a tapping plan for life for adults, videos to watch, and more. Please feel free to share with anyone you think would benefit.

The following associations offer a list of trained tapping practitioners who can assist you in your journey. Many offer virtual sessions, and many are licensed health care professionals. Search in your local area for more detail.

Evidence Based EFT (*https://evidencebasedeft.com/*) is my signature tapping training for existing health care professionals and also anyone in the community wanting to learn for themselves or to become accredited.

EFT Universe contains the archives of the international EFT community and offers training, certification, and media for learning the "evidence-based" form of EFT, called Clinical EFT. See *http:// www.eftuniverse.com*.

The Association for Comprehensive Energy Psychology provides a summary of published research and review articles in energy psychology. This summary is maintained by ACEP on their website at *www.energypsych.org.*

EFT International (previously known as AAMET International, The Association for the Advancement of Meridian Energy Techniques) is a voluntary, not-for-profit association committed to advancing and upholding the highest standards for education, training, professional development, and promotion of the skillful, creative, and ethical application of EFT. See *https://eftinternational. org/.*

Most of the organizations above have "Find a Practitioner" pages, and you can search in your country and area for someone to support your journey, should you wish.

Staying Connected

Feel free to reach out and stay connected. When we offer clinical research tapping trials, many are offered online and are free to participate, and we let you know via social media channels and my newsletter. Head over and join those to stay abreast of research that is released and calls for participants for trials.

Website: *www.petastapleton.com.*

Training in Clinical EFT website: *www.evidencebasedeft.com.*

All social media links are included there as well.

You can visit my research publications through the university site: *https://research.bond.edu.au/en/persons/peta-stapleton.*

Conclusion

In closing, my hope is that you have found a gem in this book and been able to apply tapping to an area of life for your memory. Just writing this book reminded me of the many ways tapping can assist with new learning, retrieval of stored knowledge and fact, and even lifestyle habits that can erode aspects of our recall ability. In our household we have a new student: our eldest daughter started university, and it was the perfect opportunity to show her how to tap during oral presentations for nerves (discreet tapping, of course), for exam worry, and even during lectures to stay awake! Her friends have asked her what she is doing, and now a few more students know what tapping is and what it can do. I must say I had a proud parent moment.

I always sign off when I write in a book for a reader or on a card to a customer with the words "Stay Open." You may have noticed that the phrase "stay open" has appeared throughout this book and even in the tapping examples. Tapping may be brand new in your world, or you may have been using the tool for some time. By staying open to the possibilities with tapping, you may find not only that you reduce stress in your mind and body, but that other wondrous things happen too. Here's to open minds, wonderful memories, and intact cognitive processes, everyone!

Enjoy your fantastic memory!

Chapter Notes

Chapter 1

1. Church, Dawson. 2014. *The EFT Manual* (3rd edition). Carlsbad, CA: Hay House.
2. Feinstein, David. 2012. "Acupoint stimulation in treating psychological disorders: Evidence of efficacy." *Review of General Psychology* 16, no. 4: 364–380.
3. Dhond, Rupali, Norman Kettner, and Vitaly Nadapow. 2007. "Neuroimaging acupuncture effects in the human brain." *The Journal of Alternative and Complementary Medicine* 13, no. 6: 603–616.
4. Feinstein, David. 2010. "Rapid treatment of PTSD: Why psychological exposure with acupoint tapping may be effective." *Psychotherapy: Theory, Research, Practice, Training* 47, no. 3: 385–402.
5. See https://patcarrington.com/.

Chapter 2

1. Perone, Sammy, Jeeva Palanisamy, and Stephanie M. Carlson. 2018. "Age-related change in brain rhythms from early to middle childhood: Links to executive function." *Developmental Science* 21, no. 6.
2. Arain, Mariam, Maliha Haque, Lina Johal, Puja Mathur, Wynand Nel, Afsha Rais, Ranbir Sandhu, and Sushil Sharma. 2013. "Maturation of the adolescent brain." *Neuropsychiatric Disease and Treatment* 9: 449–461.
3. Schwabe, Lars, Marian Joëls, Benno Roozendaal, Oliver T. Wolf, and Melly S. Oitzl. 2012. "Stress effects on memory: an update and integration." *Neuroscience Biobehavior Review* 36, no. 7: 1740–1749.
4. Luethi, Mathias, Beat Meier, and Carmen Sandi. 2009. "Stress effects on working memory, explicit memory, and implicit memory for neutral and emotional stimuli in healthy men." *Frontiers in Behavioral Neuroscience* 2.
5. Joëls, Marian, and Tallie Z. Baram. 2009. "The neuro-symphony of stress." *Nature Reviews Neuroscience* 10: 459–466.
6. Harvard Women's Health Watch. 2018. "Protect your brain from stress." https://www.health.harvard.edu/mind-and-mood/protect-your-brain-from-stress.
7. Walker, Pete. 2003. "Codependency, trauma and the fawn response." www.petewalker.com/codependencyFawnResponse.htm.
8. Bracha, H. Stefan. 2004. "Freeze, flight, fight, fright, faint: Adaptationist perspectives on the acute stress response spectrum." *CNS Spectrums* 9, no. 9: 679–685.
9. Bach, Donna, Gary Groesbeck, Peta Stapleton, Rebecca Sims, Katharina Blickheuser, and Dawson Church. 2019. "Clinical EFT (Emotional Freedom Techniques) improves multiple physiological markers of health." *Journal of Evidence-Based Integrative Medicine* 24.
10. Church, Dawson, Garret Yount, and Audrey J. Brooks. 2012. "The effect of Emotional Freedom Techniques on stress biochemistry: A randomized controlled trial." *The Journal of Nervous and Mental Disease* 200, no. 10: 891–6.
11. Stapleton, Peta, Gabrielle Crighton, Debbie Sabot, and Hayley Maree

161

O'Neill. 2020. "Reexamining the effect of Emotional Freedom Techniques on stress biochemistry: A randomized controlled trial." *Psychological Trauma: Theory, Research, Practice, and Policy* 12, no. 8: 869–877.

12. EFT Universe. "EFT borrowing benefits." https://www.eftuniverse.com/tutorial/borrowing-benefits.

13. Church, Dawson, Midanelle A. De Asis, and Audrey J. Brooks. 2012. "Brief group intervention using EFT (Emotional Freedom Techniques) for depression in college students: A randomized controlled trial." *Depression Research and Treatment*.

14. Chatwin, Hannah, Peta Stapleton, Brett Porter, Sharon Devine, and Terri Sheldon. 2016. "The effectiveness of Cognitive Behavioural Therapy and Emotional Freedom Techniques in reducing depression and anxiety among adults: A pilot study." *Integrative Medicine* 15, no. 2: 27–34.

Chapter 4

1. McCallion, Fiona. 2012. "Emotional Freedom Techniques for dyslexia: A case study." *Energy Psychology: Theory, Research, & Treatment* 4, no. 2.

Chapter 5

1. Harvard Health Publishing. 2010. "Preserving and improving memory as we age." https://www.health.harvard.edu/newsletter_article/preserving-and-improving-memory-as-we-age.

2. Langer, Ellen. 2009. *Counterclockwise: Mindful Health and the Power of Possibility*. New York: Ballantine Books.

Chapter 6

1. Rasch, Björn, and Jan Born. 2013. "About sleep's role in memory." *Physiological Reviews* 93, no. 2: 681–766.

2. Barnes, Jill N., and Michael J. Joyner. 2012. "Sugar highs and lows: The impact of diet on cognitive function." *The Journal of Physiology* 590, no. 12: 2831.

3. Mandolesi, Laura, Arianna Polverino, Simone Montuori, Francesca Foti, Giampaolo Ferraioli, Pierpaolo Sorrentino, and Giuseppe Sorrentino. 2018. "Effects of physical exercise on cognitive functioning and wellbeing: Biological and psychological benefits." *Frontiers in Psychology* 9, no. 509.

4. Moon, Hyo Youl, Andreas Becke, David Berron, Benjamin Becker, Nirnath Sah, Galit Benoni, Emma Janke, Susan T. Lubejko, Nigel H. Greig, Julie A. Mattison, Emrah Duzel, and Henriette van Praag. 2016. "Running-induced systemic cathepsin B secretion is associated with memory function." *Cell Metabolism* 24, no. 2: 332–340.

5. Harvard Health Publishing. 2021. "Exercise can boost your memory and thinking skills." https://www.health.harvard.edu/mind-and-mood/exercise-can-boost-your-memory-and-thinking-skills.

6. Beilharz J. E., J. Maniam, and M. J. Morris. 2016. "Short-term exposure to a diet high in fat and sugar, or liquid sugar, selectively impairs hippocampal-dependent memory, with differential impacts on inflammation." *Behavioural Brain Research* 306: 1–7.

7. Knüppel Anika, Martin J. Shipley, Clare H. Llewellyn, and Eric J. Brunner. 2017. "Sugar intake from sweet food and beverages, common mental disorder and depression: Prospective findings from the Whitehall II study." *Scientific Reports* 7, no. 6287.

Chapter 7

1. National Institute on Alcohol Abuse and Alcoholism. 2020. "Alcohol facts and statistics."

2. The Alcohol Pharmacology Education Partnership. "Alcohol, memory, and the hippocampus." https://sites.duke.edu/apep/module-3-alcohol-cell-suicide-and-the-adolescent-brain/content-alcohol-memory-and-the-hippocampus/.

3. Heffernan, T. M., T. S. O'Neill, and M. Moss. 2011. "Smoking-related prospective memory deficits in a real-world task." *Drug and Alcohol Dependence*.

4. Heffernan, Tom, and Anna-Marie Marshall. 2016. "Smoking harms not just your physical health, but your mental health too." *The Conversation*, November 24, 2016. https://theconversation.com/-smoking-harms-not-just-your-physical-health-but-your-mental-health-too-690 21.

5. Stapleton, Peta Berenice, Brett Porter, and Terri Sheldon. 2013. "Quitting smoking: How to use Emotional Freedom Techniques." *International Journal of Healing and Caring* 13, no. 1: 1–16.

6. Bach, Donna, Gary Groesbeck, Peta Stapleton, Rebecca Sims, Katharina Blickheuser, and Dawson Church. 2019. "Clinical EFT (Emotional Freedom Techniques) improves multiple physiological markers of health." *Journal of Evidence-Based Integrative Medicine* 24: 1–12.

7. Tzourio, Christophe, Carole Dufouil, Pierre Ducimetière, and Annick Alpérovitch. 1999. "Cognitive decline in individuals with high blood pressure: A longitudinal study in the elderly." *Neurology* 53, no. 9: 1948–1952.

Chapter 8

1. National Institute on Aging. 2022. "What is dementia? Symptoms, types, and diagnosis." https://www.nia.nih.gov/health/what-dementia-symptoms-types-and-diagnosis.

2. Feinstein, David. 2013. "Energy psychology treatments over a distance: The curious phenomenon of 'surrogate tapping.'" *Energy Psychology* 5, no. 1.

3. Cocker, Fiona, and Nerida Joss. 2016. "Compassion fatigue among healthcare, emergency and community service workers: A systematic review."

International Journal of Environmental Research and Public Health 13, no. 6: 618.

4. Craig, Gary, Donna Bach, Gary Groesbeck, and Daniel Benor. 2009. "Emotional Freedom Techniques (EFT) for traumatic brain injury." *International Journal of Healing and Caring* 9, no. 2: 1–12.

5. Church, Dawson, Terry Sparks, and Morgan Clond. 2016. "EFT (Emotional Freedom Techniques) and resiliency in veterans at risk for PTSD: A randomized controlled trial." *Explore: The Journal of Science and Healing* 12, no. 5: 355–365.

6. Lee, Jung Hwan, Sun Yong Chung, and Jong Woo Kim. 2015. "A comparison of Emotional Freedom Techniques-Insomnia (EFT-I) and Sleep Hygiene Education (SHE) for insomnia in a geriatric population: A randomized controlled trial." *Journal of Energy Psychology: Theory, Research, and Treatment* 7, no. 1: 22–29.

Chapter 9

1. Craig, Gary, Donna Bach, Gary Groesbeck, and Daniel J. Benor. 2009. "Emotional Freedom Techniques (EFT) for traumatic brain injury." *International Journal of Healing and Caring* 9, no. 2: 1–12.

2. Wittfoth, Dina, Antonia Pfeiffer, Michael Bohne, Heinrich Lanfermann, and Matthias Wittfoth. 2020. "Emotion regulation through bifocal processing of fear inducing and disgust inducing stimuli." *BMC Neuroscience* 21, no. 47.

3. Feinstein, David. 2013. "Energy psychology treatments over a distance: The curious phenomenon of 'surrogate tapping.'" *Energy Psychology* 5, no. 1.

Index